WHAT *IS* THE TRUTH
ABOUT WITCHCRAFT TODAY?

For centuries, organized religions have perpetuated lies about the ancient practice of Witchcraft. To this day, many misinformed people think that "Witches" worship Satan, perform human sacrifices, participate in sex orgies, and use drugs.

In *The Truth About Witchcraft Today*, Scott Cunningham puts these common misconceptions to rest by showing that Witches are women and men from all walks of life, cultural backgrounds and religious upbringings. They have found Wicca (Witchcraft) to be the only religion that encourages love for the Earth and reveres the Feminine aspect of the Divine: the Goddess—an element missing in most other religions.

If you want to know exactly how magic works, this book will inform you. Cunningham gives simple, clearcut explanations of magical practices: how a spell is cast, what a pentacle is, the difference between ritual, folk, and ceremonial magic, and more.

As this book shows, the practice of magic is *not* evil or destructive—Witches and folk magicians, through timeless rituals, are only drawing upon *natural* energies found within the Earth and our bodies to create positive, life-affirming change.

Here, then, is an excellent overview of a perennially fascinating subject—one that really does tell the truth about Witchcraft (and folk magic) today.

ABOUT SCOTT CUNNINGHAM

Scott Cunningham has been a Wiccan for more than half of his life. A chance meeting with a girl in 1971 led to his involvement in this religion. She—and other teachers after her—taught him the basics of Wicca. Along the way he also learned of the powers within herbs and stones, music, gesture and words. A published writer since 1974, he finally began merging his magical practices with his chosen profession in 1982. Many occult books have followed since then, and he's planning additional video cassette projects. Scott teaches nationwide in such places as Kansas City, Kansas, and Metairie, Louisiana when not at home in San Diego.

TO WRITE TO THE AUTHOR

We cannot guarantee that every letter written to the author can be answered, but all will be forwarded. Both the author and the publisher appreciate hearing from readers, learning of your enjoyment and benefit from this book. Llewellyn also publishes a bi-monthly news magazine with news and reviews of practical esoteric studies and articles helpful to the student, and some readers' questions and comments to the author may be answered through this magazine's columns if permission to do is included in the original letter. The author sometimes participates in seminars and workshops, and dates and places are announced in *The Llewellyn New Times*. To write to the author, or to ask a question, write to:

Scott Cunningham
c/o THE LLEWELLYN NEW TIMES
P.O. Box 64383-127, St. Paul, MN 55164-0383, U.S.A.
Please enclose a self-addressed, stamped envelope for reply, or $1.00 to cover costs.

ABOUT LLEWELLYN'S NEW AGE SERIES

The "New Age"—it's a phrase we use, but what does it mean? Does it mean that we are entering the Aquarian Age? Does it mean that a new Messiah is coming to correct all that is wrong and make Earth into a Garden? Probably not—but the idea of a *major change* is there, combined with awareness that Earth *can* be a Garden; that war, crime, poverty, disease, etc., are not necessary "evils."

Optimists, dreamers, scientists . . . nearly all of us believe in a "better tomorrow," and that somehow we can do things now that will make for a better future life for ourselves and for coming generations.

In one sense, we all know there's nothing new under the Heavens, and in another sense that every day makes a new world. The difference is in our consciousness. And this is what the New Age is all about: it's a major change in consciousness found within each of us as we learn to bring forth and manifest powers that Humanity has always potentially had.

Evolution moves in "leaps." Individuals struggle to develop talents and powers, and their efforts build a "power bank" in the Collective Unconsciousness, the soul of Humanity that suddenly makes these same talents and powers easier access for the majority.

You still have to learn the 'rules' for developing and applying these powers, but it is more like a "relearning" than a *new* learning, because with the New Age it is as if the basis for these had become genetic.

OTHER BOOKS AND PRODUCTS
BY SCOTT CUNNINGHAM

Magical Herbalism
Earth Power
Cunningham's Encyclopedia of Magical Herbs
The Magic of Incense, Oils & Brews
The Magical Household
  (co-authored with David Harrington)
*Cunningham's Encyclopedia of Crystal, Gem
  & Metal Magic*
Wicca: A Guide for the Solitary Practitioner
Magical Aromatherapy
The Magic of Food
Earth, Air, Fire & Water

Forthcoming:

Hawaiian Magic

Videos:

Herb Magic

The Truth About Witchcraft Today

by
Scott Cunningham

1992
LLEWELLYN PUBLICATIONS
St. Paul, Minnesota 55164-0383, U.S.A.

FIRST EDITION
Fourth Printing, 1992

Cover Photo: COMSTOCK, Inc./Tom Grill

Library of Congress Cataloging-in-Publication Data
Cunningham, Scott, 1956-
  The truth about witchcraft today.

  (Llewellyn's new–age series)
  This book first published in a briefer form in 1987 under title: The truth about witchcraft
  Bibliography: p.
  1. Witchcraft.   I. Cunningham, Scott, 1956–
Truth about witchcraft.   II. Title.   III. Series.
BF1566.C85   1988   133.4'3   88–45197
ISBN 0–87542–127–X (pbk.)

Llewellyn Publications
A Division of Llewellyn Worldwide, Ltd.
P.O. Box 64383, St. Paul, MN 55164-0383

Note:

This book first appeared as a 32-page pamphlet published by Llewellyn in 1987 under the title *The Truth About Witchcraft*. Because it appeared as a Llewellyn Educational Guide, I wasn't credited with writing it. After it was released, it was decided that I'd write a larger version of it. You now have it in your hands.

In this greatly expanded book we'll look at the reality of folk magic and Wicca—known to the outside world as Witchcraft. Its purpose is not to proselytize, but to discount centuries of negative propaganda and to shed some light on these still obscure subjects.

It's my hope that *The Truth About Witchcraft Today* will do its part in halting at least some of the persecution, which continues today, by those who don't understand other forms of religion and ways of life.

To all who read these words:

Bless and Blessed Be!

Table Of Contents

Part III: A Summary

Preface

Words have power. Printed words, indeed, can arouse the most potent emotions. They can excite joy, passion, peace, and rage within their readers.

For many people, ignorance is bliss. Any presentation of information contrary to their personal beliefs is heard as a cry for warfare. Censorship and book-burnings are their weapons. The "deaths" of such battles are of the mind, of freedom of thought and expression—and especially of freedom of religion.

The book you're about to read will probably be viewed by some as a weapon against reason, an intellectual step backward, an audience with—as they put it—the Devil.

It is no such thing.

Rather, this book is an introduction to Witchcraft, perhaps the least understood practice of our time. Witchcraft isn't a cauldron of human sacrifice, drugs, orgies and Devil-worship. Nor does it describe a supernatural world filled with unearthly dealings with demons.

As you will discover, Witchcraft is a way of life for hundreds of thousands—perhaps millions—of well-adjusted rational adults who simply share a view of nature that is different from that of the majority. Witchcraft is both a religion and a form of magic.

Witchcraft isn't anti-Christianity or anti-religion. In its earliest forms, it predates all present-day religions. For centuries it has been the scapegoat for the dominant religion of the Western world, a convenient answer to the ills of human life; but its adherents are not, and never were, linked in any way with the Christian summation of evil.

This book is an attempt to correct centuries of misleading, slanderous, and perverse propaganda. It is also an attempt to create a truth-based image of Witchcraft and its practitioners in the popular mind.

It isn't proselytizing, for Witchcraft isn't suited to everyone's tastes. It isn't an occult "cookbook," a ritual manual, or an expose of dark secrets. Quite simply, this is a look at the world of Witchcraft as it is today.

I've written it as a practitioner, an observer, and a researcher. From this triune viewpoint, I hope to present a balanced picture of these little-known practices.

The lies have been told. It's time for the truth.

Scott Cunningham
San Diego, California
May 10, 1988

Introduction

Night. The curtains in the upper-class home are drawn against prying eyes. Candles gleam in the living room. Incense smoke swirls. Robed figures, chanting in a long-dead language, whirl around a rustic wooden table. On it, between the candles, sit sacred images: a robust Goddess wearing a crescent Moon on Her forehead, a God holding a spear in His upraised hand.

All movement stops. A woman standing near the altar says:

> In this sacred space and time
> We call now the Old Ones:
> The Goddess of the Moon, of seas
>   and rivers;
> The God of the rayed Sun, of valleys
>   and forests:
> Draw near us during this, our circle.

This is Witchcraft.

Two thousand miles away, a fifteen-year-old girl affixes a green candle onto a Polaroid photo of a friend. In the darkened room she lights the candle. She closes her eyes. Within her mind, she visualizes a glowing purple light surrounding her boyfriend's broken arm. She chants an impassioned healing incantation.

This, too, is Witchcraft.

These examples sum up Witchcraft. It is a religion known as Wicca. It is also the practice of folk magic.

Thanks to a centuries-long smear campaign, the average person thinks that Witchcraft consists of Satanic worship, orgies, and drug use. They falsely believe Witches to practice a mishmash of Devil worship, unsavory rituals, cruelty, and human sacrifice.

Persons who practice such atrocities certainly do exist: murderers, psychotics, and those frustrated by the religion into which they were born. But these people *aren't* Witches, and they *don't* practice Witchcraft.

It isn't surprising that such false beliefs exist, for they've been reinforced by literature, the fine arts, motion pictures, television, and tens of thousands of hours of virulent sermons. Though the facts have been readily available for the past twenty years or so, they've been largely suppressed, ridiculed, or ignored.

As is often the case, the truth about Witchcraft is far less tantalizing than the lies. It doesn't lend itself as readily to talk shows as Satanism and rarely creates headline news.

But it is there.

Folk Magic

Folk magic is just that—the magic of the people. Long ago, practicing simple magical rituals was as normal as eating or sleeping. Magic was a part of daily existence. To question its effectiveness, or indeed its necessity, was tantamount to a 20th-century person questioning whether the Earth is round.

Though times have changed, contemporary practitioners of folk magic accept the same principles and perform rituals similar to those of bygone eras.

Folk magicians don't use supernatural powers. They're not out to control the world. They aren't dangerous or evil. They simply sense and utilize natural energies which have not yet been quantified, codified, and accepted into the hallowed halls of science.

These energies spring from the Earth itself, not from demons or Satan. They're present within stones, colors, and herbs, as well as within our own bodies. Through timeless rituals, folk magicians rouse, release, and direct these energies for the purpose of creating positive, specific, needed change.

To the atheist, using these energies is no more absurd than the act of praying. To the materialist, this practice overlooks the monetary value of the Earth. To the Christian, who has been taught to "dominate and subdue" the Earth, such intimate connection with nature and its tangible effects is dangerous, evil.

All three viewpoints are, perhaps, correct to their holders—but not to folk magicians. Once again, folk magicians have bypassed traditional, orthodox religion that states that power is in the hands of "God" and His priests, saints, and earthly representatives. They have gone further than the materialists in recognizing the qualities of nature. And they—in common with many others—simply don't worry what atheists think.

Folk magicians are persons who, unsatisfied by religious or physically based creeds, have investigated the Earth and its treasures. They've gone within themselves to sense the mystic powers of the human body and to feel its connections with the Earth.

And they have discovered that magic works.

Wicca

Wicca is a contemporary religion. Its practitioners revere the Goddess and God as the creators of the universe—as tangible, conscious beings. Though in general Wiccans don't subscribe to one specific form, they accept reincarnation and magic, revere the Earth as a manifestation of the Goddess and God, and meet for religious ceremony at times appointed by the Moon and Sun.

Wicca is nonproselytizing. It is life-affirming, not death-dealing. It has its own set of myths, religious objects, rituals, and laws, many of which bear little resemblance to those of other present-day religions.

Wiccans may be female or male, of any age or race. They may meet in groups of up to fifty or more, in cozy covens of thirteen or less, or may worship the Goddess and God alone. Though most speak English, they may call the Deities in Spanish, French, Welsh, Swedish, Scottish Gaelic, German, Dutch, and in many other languages. As a religion, Wicca exists throughout Europe; in all fifty of the United States; in Central and South America; in Australia; in Japan, and elsewhere.

Wicca isn't an organized religion in the sense that Christianity is organized, but national groups do exist within the U.S. for the purposes of protecting Wiccans from legal, literary, and physical abuse. Some forms of Wicca have been recognized by the federal government as legitimate religious groups.

Wiccans are women and men of every profession, cultural background, and religious upbringing. For many of them Wicca is the only religion they've found that encourages love for the Earth and it's inhabitants (human, animal, and vegetable), and that promotes the practice of folk magic to transform their lives into positive experiences. Women, especially, are drawn to it because of its acceptance of the feminine aspect of Divinity—the Goddess. For Wiccans, theirs is the only religion that allows a truly intimate link with Deity.

Wiccans aren't organizing to rule the world or to overthrow Christianity, despite the frenzied lies that are daily broadcasted by televangelists. Its adherents aren't out on the streets or on the phones ready to accept converts. Indeed, most Wiccans are intelligent enough to realize that their religion isn't the only path to Deity—a trait shared with few members of other religions.

But for them, it's the right path.

§ ——

PART I

FOLK MAGIC

—— §

1

The Magic Of The People

Folk magic was born in an age of wonder. Tens of thousands of years ago, nature was a mysterious force. Points of light swung far overhead in the sky. Invisible energies ruffled matted hair and kicked up dust storms. Water fell from above. Powerful forces, inconceivable to those early humans, sent flashes of light from the clouds, blasting trees into raging infernos. Women miraculously bore young. Blood was sacred. Food was sacred. Water, the Earth, plants, animals, the wind, and all that existed was infused with power.

Magic—as well as religion and science—sprang from the actions of the first humans who attempted to understand, contact, and gain some control over such forces. Through countless centuries they examined the natural world around them, discovering the physical properties of water, fire, plants, and animals. They investigated the mysterious processes of birth and death, and pondered where the deceased had "gone."

They marvelled at the intricate patterns of minerals and flowers, and watched the clouds moving overhead.

These earlier peoples were different from us. They lived in and with nature, depending upon it for their sustenance as well as for protection against human and animal dangers. When they reaped wild grains for food, smelled richly scented flowers, or brought glistening, opalescent shells up from the ocean's edge, they must have sensed that there was something more to these things than their solid, physical forms.

Unhindered by materialistic training, their primeval minds explored the world and discovered an indescribable *something* existing within all objects and beings. In inanimate objects the color, form, size, and weight may have been recognized as clues to their nonphysical natures. The location in which an object was found—beside streams, high on mountains, or deep within the Earth—may also have been an indicator of the type of energy found within it.

The powers that seemed to be afoot in human beings were of incredible diversity. A man filled with tenderness radiated different energy than one bent on killing. A strong, healthy individual's energies were similarly strong and healthy, while the sick had lowered reserves of a lesser type. Even the bones of the dead, along with her or his personal belongings (if any), were also sensed to contain a form of power.

Eventually, ritual was developed as a means of contacting and utilizing the energy within humans as well as in the natural world. How, why, or where this happened is of little importance, but this step marked the advent of magic and religion.

Yes, religion. Speculation exists today that the earliest humans held some type of spiritual reverence. They certainly practiced magic, and in earlier times the two were intimately linked—as they continue to be (See Chapter Five).

Certain objects prized for their energies were probably utilized for specific ends. Amber, not a true mineral but a fossilized pine resin, may have been among the first materials used for magical purposes. Images of bears and geometric carvings of amber—often perforated for hanging purposes—apparently were worn as protective or hunt-ensuring devices in the earliest ages.

Pieces of meteoric iron must have been viewed with awe, especially if the falling of the meteor had been witnessed. Flowers used for magical and ritual purposes were held in higher esteem once their medicinal properties had been recognized.

Thus folk magic slowly developed into a method of using natural objects in ritual ways for specific, necessary purposes such as protection, fertility, safe childbirth, and successful hunts.

At some point human energies were introduced into folk magic. Complicated rituals developed as a means of uniting the magician with the object's energy. In a sense, this was a form of communication. Gesture, rhythm, dance, ritual postures, and later, hallucinogenic plants, were used to successfully merge human energy with that of prized objects.

All magical systems and religions grew from these early practices. Tribal magic, as well as group religious rituals, undoubtedly developed from folk magic, but the magic of the individual survived.

These simple rituals continued to be used for many thousands of years. As great civilizations rose and fell—Sumer, Egypt, Babylon, Greece, Crete, and Rome—folk magic continued to be practiced, while priests and priestesses slaved over state religions and magical systems.

Then a new organized religion, born in the Near East after the death of a Jewish prophet, flexed its growing political muscles. The official conversion of the Roman empire to Christianity around 325 C.E. (Common Era) spread Christianity throughout the Western world. As country after country converted, many of the old ways of folk magic were forgotten, often under threat of imprisonment or death.

Some peoples, unwilling to discard thousand-year-old rituals, altered them slightly to conform to the new religion. That magic which could not be made to at least vaguely conform was practiced in secret. The days when the old European charms and spells were a part of everyday life were over.

The leaders of the new religion, determined to wield absolute control over all aspects of human life, sought to stamp out such "crimes" as foretelling the future, psychic healing, the creation of protective amulets and love-attracting charms, and everything else which failed to fit in with this religion's creed. Throughout the "known" world folk magic became a dim memory, as scenes of religious mass murders (performed in the name of God) became commonplace.

Soon after, the advent of modern scientific inquiry occurred. As the horrors of the Medieval and Renaissance Witch persecutions faded from memory, humans began investigating the ways of nature in a new light.

Magnetism, medicine and surgery, mathematics, and astronomy were codified and moved from the realm of "superstition" and magic to science.

Building upon this knowledge, the Industrial Revolution began in the late 19th century. Humans gained some control over the Earth through mechanistic means. Machines soon replaced religion in overcoming folk magic. Humans, no longer dependent upon the Earth for their lives, grew isolated from their planet.

In the 1900s a series of local and world wars ripped apart much of what remained of the old ways of living for millions of Europeans, Americans, Asians, and Pacific Islanders. Folk magic, once the lifeblood of all humans, had never seen darker days.

But it had not completely died out. Wherever machines and technology hadn't yet invaded, folk magic continued to exist: in areas of Asia, Africa, and the South Pacific; in Central and South America; in rural sections of North America such as the Ozarks; in Hawaii; and even in parts of Europe.

During the 1960s folk magic sprang back to life. The youth movement in the United States and Britain rebelled against rigid social codes and Christian-based ideals. Some young persons turned to Buddhism, Zen, and other Eastern teachings. Others became enchanted with what little they could learn of spells, charms, herb magic, tarot cards, amulets, and talismans. Countless popular books and articles appeared, revealing this once-public knowledge to a new generation dissatisfied with their purely technological lives.

Spellbooks and magical texts, written by researchers or practitioners of folk magic, were purchased by persons whose ancestors had originated these practices. Books such as Paul Huson's *Mastering Witchcraft*, Kathryn Paulsen's *The Complete Book of Magic and Witchcraft*, and Raymond Buckland's *Practical Candleburning*—along with dozens of others—were hugely successful. A reawakening had begun.

But the religious suppression of folk magic continued unabated during the 1960s. Books were released stating that this renewed interest in folk magic (usually referred to as Witchcraft) heralded the end of the world. Preachers in the United States publicly burned occult books and magical objects. They did this, they said, in an attempt to destroy "the Devil's works."

However, Christianity's influence in shaping public opinion was weakening. Though many nonpractitioners continued to view magic as Satanic, unnatural and dangerous, open-minded persons investigated it for themselves. Some become ardent practitioners, finding in folk magic a link with their ancestors and a sense of personal power.

Today, the resurgence begun in the late 1960s has produced a generation of aware individuals. Many of these folk magicians have also become involved in channelling, psychic healing, herbal medicine, sensory deprivation, holistic consciousness, crystal work, vegetarianism, neurolinguistic programming, meditation, and Eastern teachings. This—along with a big media push—has produced the New Age movement.

As a response to the continuing interest in folk magic and non-Christian spirituality, and to the waning of Christianity's social power, orthodox religion has now turned its propaganda guns toward this new wave of folk magic by again predicting that these are the last days of our planet.

I've included this short, greatly condensed history of folk magic in Europe and the U. S. to point out that it is nothing new. It has been with us almost as long as we've been on the Earth. Exactly what it is will be explored in the next few chapters, but what it *isn't* is almost as important as what it is.

Folk magic isn't "the Devil's work." It isn't Satanism. It doesn't involve living sacrifices. It doesn't consist of talking to spirits or bondage to demons. It isn't dark, dangerous, evil or supernatural. Folk magic isn't anti-Christian, anti-religion or anti-anything.

Folk magic is pro-life, pro-love, pro-healing. It is a tool with which people transform their lives. It is a relationship with the Earth. When "normal" means failure, when all efforts have brought no results, many millions today turn to folk magic.

It is practiced by twelve-year-old girls and senior men and women. All kinds of women and men—professionals, laborers, lawyers, and salespersons—perform spells. Persons of every race carry out ancient rituals, some of which may be linked with their cultural background. A Chicana living in southwestern Arizona might brush her children with rue and rosemary leaves as part of a healing ritual. A Cajun man might stop by a New Orleans shop to purchase a green candle and money-drawing incense in preparation for a wealth-attracting ritual. Rational Hawaiians place leaves of a certain plant in elevators to guard women against rape.

For those with no strong attachments to their ancestors, a plethora of spells and rituals are available for use in personal magic.

Folk magic, then, constitutes the bulk of ancient and modern magical practices performed by individuals to improve their lives. Unfettered by social beliefs or religious strictures, folk magicians carve their own futures through timeless rituals.

Folk magic is alive once again.

2

The Spell

The spell is at the heart of folk magic. It is simply a ritual in which various tools are purposefully used, the goal is fully stated (in words, pictures or within the mind), and energy is moved to bring about the needed result.

Spells can be as simple as reciting a short chant over a fresh rose while placing it between two pink candles in order to draw love; forming and retaining an image of the needed result in the mind; or placing a quartz crystal in a sunny window for protective purposes.

Spells are usually misunderstood by nonpractitioners. In popular thought, all you need to perform magic is a spell—a *real* spell, not the kind you find in books: a spell passed from an angel to King Solomon, a spell inscribed in some mythological sixteenth-century Welsh Witch's workbook—a spell of untold power. Your wildest dreams could be fulfilled if only you had a real spell.

Many seem to think that simply by gathering together a few objects (the stranger the better) and chanting a few words, the powers of the universe will spark and move and produce miracles. This is the product of a world that believes magic to be supernatural, irrational, impossible.

But magic works with nature, with natural energies. The spells—chants, gestures with tools, lighting of candles—are the outer form and they are worthless unless energy is moved. This is the sole responsibility of the magician. No demonic power flows to help the spell-caster. Instead the magician, by correctly performing a spell, builds up what I call "personal power." At the proper time this power is released to go to work in manifesting the spell.

Effective spells—or rather, spells that will produce the needed results—are designed to bring this about. In the days when magic was a part of the everyday routine, spells were probably pedestrian. The magician knew that the ritual would work and didn't need to be coaxed into this belief.

After the glory days of magic this natural approach to magic was gone. For spells to be effective magicians had to lay aside their culturally ingrained disbelief. The very nature of spells changed. The magician donned special clothing which symbolized the event about to occur. Candles were lit and incense burned to produce the proper romantic atmosphere. The spell might have been worked exactly at midnight in a desolate area with the Full Moon shining far above. Strange words were chanted to stir the power within the magician. Finally, after an hour or so of working up to the proper peak of energy as well as to the prerequisite state of mind, the magician simply released the power and the spell was finished.

Chants, candles, incense, and even the Moon contain specific energies which can be utilized in magic, but such tools aren't necessary to the performance of folk magic. The magic is in the magician, not within the tools.

Strange trappings and bizarre ingredients aren't necessary either—unless the magician deems them to be. Different types of folk magicians use different types of spells. If of an analytical, intellectual mind, the folk magician may prefer visualization rituals in which the goal is firmly established in the mind as a vehicle through which the power will flow. A more romantic magician may prefer herbs, crystals, and candles. Those intrigued with form and intricate patterns may find that the use of runes, images, colors, and magical symbols fulfills their needs. Artists may create ritual paintings; musicians, spell-songs.

This is mere generalization, but it should serve to show that no one type of spell will be equally effective in every folk magician's hands. Additionally, all spells—published or not—can be effective.

Spells are designed to release personal power within the magician. It is this energy—along with natural objects such as crystals, herbs, oils, incense and the like—that powers the spell, that gets it moving. How does it work? We can't fully explain it yet, but the following theory seems valid:

There is a power in the universe. It is the power of life. This is the inexplicable force behind the wonders that early humans encountered. The Earth, the solar system, the stars—all that is manifest—is a product of this power. Humans have given the names of "God" and "Goddess" to this energy source. It is that which is worshipped in every religion in various forms.

This is the power that keeps our bodies alive, that allows us to reproduce, that is within all beings and things. It isn't supernatural; on the contrary, this is the power of nature itself.

Human beings are manifestations of this power, as are plants, rocks, trees, clouds, and water. Our bodies aren't power plants as much as they're power-assimilators. We take in energy from the food and drink that we consume, from the Sun and Air. We release it during exercise and any physical activity (including sex), and during concentration, prayer, and magic.

Therefore, magic can be seen as a method of releasing personal power. It is as real and natural as exercising or making love. And just as those two activities are engaged in for specific purposes, so too is magic.

Personal power isn't the sole source of energy used in folk magic. It is usually combined with that of various objects such as herbs and stones, which have been used in folk magic for countless generations. These things, to the folk magician, aren't viewed as merely pretty rocks or fragrant plants, but as energy sources.

This power can be roused and concentrated. Personal power—that which exists within humans—is "awakened" through music or chanting; through dance; through manipulation of various objects; through concentration or magical visualization.

Energies within stones, herbs, and other objects

are roused with rituals. Herbs may be blessed or visualized to contain the energies. Stones may be placed between the palms. During such operations the magician senses the energies within these objects, touches them in a metaphysical sense, and sets them stirring.

Humans and natural objects contain bands or spectrums of different types of energy. Only one type of energy exists, but the physical form in which it is manifest determines its specific characteristics. Thus the herb rosemary contains energies that can be used for a variety of magical purposes.

The type of energy within our bodies is constantly changing in accordance with our thoughts, hopes, wishes, and physical condition.

This power can be "programmed" or "fine-tuned" to effect a specific result. This programming is accomplished within the magician as well as in the natural objects used in the spell. This usually occurs after the magician has sensed the energies within her/himself and those objects to be used, if any. These energies are then narrowed down to the spell's purpose, such as love, money, or healing.

This process may entail visualization: creating and holding certain images or concepts in the mind. Color is another tool often used to program the energy: a rose about to be used in a love-attraction ritual may be seen to be emanating a brilliant pink, which is the love hue.

When the energies to be used in the spell are at the proper pitch and frequency (to borrow those terms), all is ready for the actual transference.

During this attuning process candles may be lit,

symbols scratched or drawn onto birch bark, or words stated, but such ritual actions only serve to intensify the magician's concentration on the work at hand.

This power can be moved and directed. The attuned power can be freed from its physical confines (the human body, quartz crystals, etc.) and sent out toward the spell's goal. During healing rituals it is projected toward the sick person. If protection is needed, the energy might be directed into a small object that can be worn, into an area of a building such as the front door, or even into a car or pet.

Once the energy has been freed from its material forms, it is no longer bound by physical laws. The folk magician can move it ten feet or ten thousand miles to do its work. The folk magician's knowledge and experience—not the distance involved—determines the spell's effectiveness.

The energy is moved through the use of visualization, through ritual gestures such as pointing fingers, through use of wands, swords and magical knives— or simply through concentration.

This power, once moved, has an effect on its target. Because everything that exists contains greater or lesser amounts of the same divine energy, everything can be affected by the introduction of similar energies. This principle is the fulcrum of folk magic, the basic thrust of the process itself; for if the power is acknowledged to exist, if it can be charged with specific types of purposes and be moved, then unless it has an effect once it reaches its destination, all is for naught.

The method by which the power changes its target is either determined by the magician during the ritual or is left up to circumstances at the time of its arrival.

Exactly *how* this change takes place cannot be explained—at least not yet. Perhaps it can be understood by using an analogy: when a few drops of food coloring are added to a glass of water, the water itself hasn't been dramatically altered; but the introduction of the food coloring, which is soluble in water, has created a blend of both substances—color and water.

Magic seems to work along the same lines. Healing energy sent to a sick or wounded person doesn't actually heal, but seems to kick the body's healing processes into high gear. Protective energy doesn't visually alter the building or object in which it is infused, but it does create a nonphysical change—an energy barrier that resists the entrance of dangerous or negative powers.

That, in short, is at least one folk magician's rationale of magic. Not all magicians would subscribe to every detail of this model, but it gives us a framework from which we can create our own explanations.

Examined from this vantage point, folk magic cannot and could not be construed as a supernatural, otherworldly process. Though we haven't yet explained every intricacy of folk magic (fringe physics is coming close to this achievement), it's a perfectly natural process that most of us simply haven't used.

The spell is a form of ritual drama—a series of physical, mental, and magical actions designed to rouse, program, release, and direct magical energy for a specific purpose.

Science doesn't pretend to have penetrated every secret of this mysterious force. The effects of turning on a light switch would have seemed magical to our predecessors, and still is to some. "Turning on" magical power, once commonplace, is today an occult (hidden) practice, but it occurs many thousands of times a day.

Once a newspaper reporter complained that magic, as I explained it, was too ordinary, too everyday. Looking for screaming headlines and demon devotionals, he was crestfallen to discover that magic is a natural process.

I didn't mind disappointing him. *Magic is the movement of natural energies.* All the trappings, the secrecy, the bat's blood and newt's eyes, the chilling music, strange incantations and the like are there for those persons who need or want them—those who can't feel the energy within themselves or within nature without dramatic props to suspend their disbelief.

True folk magic, as we've seen, doesn't require them. All it requires is a human being with magical knowledge and deep connections with the Earth. Within these things are all the secrets of magic.

Another important point, often overlooked in books, should be made regarding folk magic: belief doesn't empower spells. I may believe that alien beings from another planet landed in 1939 and dictated battle plans to Adolf Hitler. Of course, I'm not certain that this is true because I have no proof.

Belief is uncertainty and implies that the believer may be incorrect. It is a crutch, an idea which often has nothing but emotion to back it up. A belief in God is one thing; the knowledge of a personal relationship with Him or Her is quite another.

Belief may play a part in magic at the onset of a person's experiences in it. This is a necessary step. Eventually, once magic has proven to be effective, this belief firms into certain knowledge. Belief isn't enough and faith isn't enough. Only knowledge leads to effective magic: the knowledge that magic is a genuine process—that energy is a viable, natural part of life, and can be programmed and projected to produce specific effects.

So those books that say the magician must *believe* in magic for it to be effective are incorrect. Belief is no more a part of magic than it is part of computer repair. Once a person has mastered the basics, she or he knows that if certain steps are taken, certain effects will be achieved.

Folk magicians have no doubt regarding the efficacy of their magic. They know that spells are keys to unlocking natural energies that can be utilized to improve their lives.

3

Tools Of Power

Although personal power—that which resides within humans—is the most potent force at work in folk magic, its practitioners utilize a wide variety of magical objects borrowed from the spells and rituals of various cultures. Such "tools" are used to lend their own energies, as well as to produce the state of consciousness necessary for magical workings.

Magic can be, and often is, effective purely on a personal level, with the magician utilizing no power other than that which resides within. However, folk magicians have always used natural objects as well as expertly crafted tools to strengthen their magical rituals.

Here are some of them.

Crystals

The use of crystals and stones is perhaps the latest rediscovery of ancient folk magic. Countless books have been published on the subject, and many persons are now working with the magic of stones and discovering their abilities to improve their lives.

This widespread interest isn't difficult to explain. While crystals are certainly beautiful and possess intrinsic values, they also contain specific energies available for magical use. Stones have been utilized in magic since the earliest times, and with herbs, may have been the first magical tools.

Step into any New Age store and your eyes will be dazzled by a wide variety of crystals. Quartz crystal predominates and is found in dozens of specific structures and forms: double-terminated, castellated, anhydrous, phantom, red phantom, laser wands, and tabular are some currently prized shapes.

Colored varieties of quartz are also used in magic, such as amethyst (purple), carnelian (orange), citrine (yellowish), blue quartz, rose quartz, and so on.

Besides quartz, dozens of other types of stones are being used to promote health, draw love, attract money, bring peace, and to guard against ills of every kind. Many persons aren't aware that quartz crystal isn't the only type of stone called upon to release or to absorb energy.

Perhaps one hundred or more stones are currently being used in magic. Some have only recently been rediscovered. Fluorite, a stone virtually unknown outside mineralogical circles until quite recently, is now widely used to promote mental activity. Sugilite, a beautiful purplish stone, has been found to promote psychism and spirituality, and is commonly used to speed healing. Clear, lavender-hued kunzite promotes peace and healing. Tourmaline is garnering its share of magical uses as well.

Folk magicians arouse, program, release, and direct the energies within stones. They don't simply pick one up and demand that it do its work; they work with these tools of the Earth.

Once empowered, folk magicians use stones in various ritual ways. They're worn, carried, slipped under the mattress, or placed on magical altars. Crystals are stroked onto the body and placed in the home to release their beneficial energies. They may also be combined with other tools, such as herbs and candles, in various manners during spells.

What do you feel when you think of diamonds? Or emeralds? Sapphires? Rubies? Do you associate them with greed? A lost—or found—love? Do you simply want to own them? We have formed certain associations with diamonds and other precious stones because of their monetary value and frequent use in wedding and engagement rings.

Some folk magicians certainly share such feelings, but those who've worked with stones see them in far different ways. Diamonds are stones of strength, reconciliation, healing, and protection; emeralds—love, money, health, and psychic powers; sapphires—meditation, peace, and power; rubies—joy, wealth, and restful sleep.

Crystals have become big business, as more individuals turn to them for their beauty and energies. They're the material signature of the New Age as well as ancient tools of folk magic.

Herbs

Arguably, herbs were first used in magic and religion long before they were thrown into cooking pots for culinary or medicinal purposes. Today they've been rediscovered by new generations of folk magicians who're busy collecting, mixing, smoldering, and brewing these fragrant treasures.

Herbs, like crystals, possess specific, distinct energies that are utilized in magic. Rose petals may be strewn around the home to promote peace. They may also be placed between pink candles to bring love into the folk magician's life. Cinnamon may be burned to stimulate intelligence; lavender flowers added to the bath for purificatory purposes; and sandalwood burned to heighten meditation and psychic experiences.

An incredible variety of herbs—encompassing fruits, trees, flowers, roots, nuts, seeds, seaweeds, ferns, grasses, and all other types of plant materials—is used in folk magic. This is one form of magic that we haven't quite forgotten, for we still give flowers to loved ones, splash on plant-based perfumes and colognes to attract mates, serve herb-enhanced meals to possible lovers (or receive them).

Herbs may be burned as incense to release their energies into the air, or carried in the pocket and sprinkled in the home for various magical purposes. Their oil forms may also be used. Essential oils and magical blends are rubbed onto the body or candles, are added to the bath, or used to anoint crystals and other objects in ritual settings.

Once the province of every wisewoman and country magician, herbs have again been grasped as tools of power by many folk magicians.

Candles And Colors

Candles used to be a necessity for nighttime light.

Today they've become luxuries in many homes. Folk magicians use candles as focal points for power, as well as for the additional magical energy that issues from their colors and flames.

Candles of specific shapes are sometimes burned during ritual, with the shape corresponding to a needed magical goal. More frequently, however, the candle is a simple taper, as it's the color—not shape—that is of importance during folk magic rituals.

Colors have strong effects on our unconscious minds as well as on our bodies. This is currently being accepted by psychologists who have pioneered studies in this area. Prison walls are painted pink to calm disturbed, violent prisoners. Hospital rooms are often soft shades of blue or green to stimulate healing and to minimize the trauma of surgery. Red is used in advertising and packaging to attract attention, just as it is used on stop signs and on flashing emergency lights.

Folk magicians, knowing that color has magical as well as psychological effects, select colored candles that are in harmony with their magical need. Here's a quick list:

> *White:* Purification, protection, peace
> *Red:* Protection, strength, health, courage, exorcism, passion
> *Black:* Negation, absorption of disease and negativity
> *Blue:* Healing, psychism, patience, happiness
> *Green:* Finances, money, fertility, growth, employment
> *Yellow:* Intelligence, theorization, divination

Brown: Healing (of animals), homes, housing
Pink: Love, friendships
Orange: Adaptability, stimulation, attraction
Purple: Power, healing (of severe disease),
    spirituality, meditation

Candles are rubbed with fragrant oils and surrounded by crystals. Herbs may be piled up around their bases or scattered onto the working area. Various symbols could be scratched onto their surfaces. The tapers may be placed in certain patterns or in special candleholders.

As the candle flames, the folk magician visualizes her or his need. The flame directs the personal power as well as that of the objects placed around it.

Despite early horror stories, candles aren't burned upside down. They aren't made of human tallow. These are lies spread by nonpractitioners in the seemingly endless war between orthodox religion and folk magic.

Candles are used as magical tools. Their strong effects on the conscious mind can easily be tested. Simply buy a white candle. While alone in a darkened or completely dark room, place it in a holder and light its wick. As the match flares up and ignites the wick, settle down before it. Still your mind and watch the flame as it slowly melts the wax. Breathe softly, slowly, gazing at the candle like a mystic into a crystal sphere.

Assuming that you're uninterrupted, you'll probably find yourself in a slightly different state of mind. You may be more relaxed, less stressed, at peace. When you turn on the light this mood may vanish like darkness at sunrise, but you'll have experienced one of the most powerful effects of candles: their ability to alter our conscious minds. They allow us to shut out the technological world and attune to ancient times when human-created fire was the ultimate tool of technology—to an age where magic was as real as birth and death.

This isn't magic, but preparation for magic. Though candles contain energies (related to color), they're primarily tools that facilitate consciousness shifts. They also serve as focal points for personal and natural power. Folk magicians have used candles (as well as their predecessors, torches and oil lamps) for millenia.

The simplest form of ritual which could be deemed part of folk magic (as opposed to purely mental magic) could consist of lighting an appropriately colored candle, rousing personal power, programming it with the need, then releasing and directing it into the candle's flame. All this is done while visualizing the needed outcome.

This may be the reason why candles are lit in a million spells every day around the world.

Chants, Words, And Poetry

The breath, as well as the sounds formed with it, is an integral part of folk magic.

To the ancient Hawaiians, the power used in magic was known as *mana*. Every aspect of nature and the human body—especially the breath—was infused with *mana*. Thus chants were carefully stated during spells and rituals, for the words themselves contained the power of breath. This same idea is found the world over, and may have originated in prehistoric times.

When speech had developed to the point where it gained prominence over earlier methods of communication, such as grunts, bodily postures and hand gestures, it was probably used for magical and ritual purposes.

Humans have given the spoken word tremendous importance in both the material and magical realms. Through the ages, words of power and secret chants have been passed down from one folk magician to another. Until the late 1900s, British wisewomen preserved short, rhyming charms aimed at stopping bleeding or cooling fevers. Oaths are still sworn with words, and lying (especially face-to-face) is considered the ultimate insult and disgrace in many parts of the world.

In human relations, words are the primary means of communication. For illiterate persons (of whom millions exist in the U.S. alone), it is the only intelligible method of sharing emotions, thoughts, and experiences.

In magic words can be used as a form of communication between the folk magician and the power within. Words are spoken to herbs, candles, and stones, especially during rituals designed to arouse and program their energies. The words themselves aren't usually thought to create the necessary changes, though the interplay of vibrations (sound waves) with physical objects may be a factor. Rather, words are used to help pinpoint the magician's concentration and to allow her or him to perform this magical action. In other words, when a folk magician speaks to a candle, she or he is actually speaking to the self.

Poetry is perhaps the most potent form of ritual

speech. It touches and speaks to the unconscious mind, the mind of dreams, psychism, sleep, and magic. Rhymed words are easier to recall, and flow smoothly during ritual operations. Hence they've long been used in spells.

The importance of the words used lie in their ability to imbue the folk magician with the proper state of mind, and once this has been achieved, allow him or her to move energy. Ancient words of power may be ineffective if they're meaningless to the magician. A freshly composed, four-line rhyme—if it speaks to the magician—can be sufficient to produce the necessary state of mind and to get the power flowing.

The power of words, the whisper of breath, and the undeniable effect of sound are ancient magical tools.

Many other techniques and objects are used by folk magicians. These include: knots—used to represent the physical manifestation of a spell or to lend protection to a person or place; clay—which can be molded into symbolic shapes; mirrors—used to reflect negativity ("evil") and to awaken psychic awareness; sand—which is poured into specific images, somewhat like the way the Navajo create sand paintings; water—a tool of purification; runes—ancient or modern symbols containing within their few lines specific magical energies; ink—used to create shapes or to sketch runes; and food—which is prepared or cooked and eaten for specific magical changes.

Many spells and rituals utilize two or more of the four basic tools explored in this chapter. A simple peace-inducing ritual, for example, may involve *blue candles, amethyst,* a handful of *rose petals,* and a peaceful *chant.* These are used in appropriate ways by the folk magician to achieve the necessary results.

The tools of folk magic are as normal as the stones beneath our feet, the candles on our dinner tables, and the herbs growing in our gardens and parks. It is only through magical ritual that these everyday objects become instruments of power in the hands of folk magicians.

4

Harm None

On a deserted mountaintop a lone folk magician mixes warmed beeswax with rue, rosemary, and myrrh oil. Bending over her work, she pulls, smooths, and molds the mixture into a rough human shape. Twenty minutes later she has successfully captured the image of a local woman—the curve of the hips, the long nose, the stringy hair.

The Moon rises in the East as the Sun sets. The Witch lights a small fire of rowan and elder twigs and throws a sprinkling of sandalwood chips onto the flames. As she places the image beside the blaze, scented smoke rises and surrounds the folk magician's face. Her eyes drill into the warming image as she intently visualizes.

She slowly lifts her arms, feeling the power rise within her. After a few moments the Witch suddenly points her fingers at the image. A tremendous, awesome rush of energy streams from them into the little wax doll. Certain that the power has been sent into the image, and thus into the woman which it represents, the folk magician picks up the doll and walks home.

Her healing spell has ended.

One of the most prevalent charges brought against folk magicians and Witches is that they spend most of their time sticking pins into dolls. They delight, outsiders say, in throwing around hexes and curses with the purpose of injuring, controlling, sickening, and killing human beings.

Perhaps in the 50,000 or more years that folk magic has been practiced there were a few who attempted to perform such deeds, but during that same time millions of outright murders have been committed by priests, monks, kings, queens, judges, juries, mayors, police chiefs, and a plethora of common folk of every religious background. Many of the most brutal, horrendous, and widespread acts of genocide were—and still are—being practiced by religious factions.

Folk magicians don't use magic for this purpose. This is not to say that, with a little searching, a person who claims to practice magic might be found who will agree to perform a death hex or some such ritual; but hit men and political assassins of every religious background can also be found.

If we accept the fact that the majority of persons who own firearms are not and will not become murderers, we must also accept the fact that most folk magicians don't use their talents for this end.

Surprised? It may be surprising because usually we assume that anyone with power—spiritual or temporal—will abuse it to the limits of their capabilities. In the United States we've seen political power abused by the White House, religious power abused by televangelists and small-town preachers, and legal power abused by judges and lawyers. Wouldn't folk magicians also abuse their power?

No. The majority of experienced folk magicians—not dabblers—realize that misusing magic isn't the way. They don't believe that our problems are caused by others, and that by eliminating somebody, our lives become paradises.

Folk magicians realize that we create our futures every second that we live. Today's decisions can have far-reaching effects on our lives. If we allow others to manipulate us, if we allow ourselves to marry someone we don't love, if we allow ourselves to ruin our lives, then we have only ourselves to blame, not others.

Thus, the motivation for folk magicians to harm or kill others through magic is nonexistent. In addition, folk magicians largely subscribe to a code of magical morality, which kills off any spiritual violence that they may wish to do during fits of emotional turmoil.

If magicians perform effective magic, it follows that they must ensure the proper use of this power. Because folk magicians utilize the energy of their own bodies and also that of the Earth, they realize that this energy is greater than themselves. Even folk magicians with no religious or spiritual feelings—for folk magic isn't truly religious in nature—sense responsibility in wielding this power.

The power at work in folk magic is just that—power. It is neither positive nor negative, neither good nor evil. It is the intention and goal of the magician working with it that determines whether this energy is used for helpful or harmful ends.

Folk magicians usually perform magic for positive reasons. Certainly, it's untrue to say that *all* practitioners use folk magic in nonharmful ways, just as the statement "all politicians use their influence for the greater good" is untrue. However, those few practitioners of harmful magic are violating the basic principle of folk magic:

Harm None

This premise, the idea behind most religious and civil codes of conduct, is universal. *Harm none* means just that—not yourself, not your enemies—none. Harming here includes physical, emotional, mental, spiritual, and psychic damage. Manipulation of others (such as forcing someone to fall in love with you) is also taboo, as is harming the Earth and its treasures.

The so-called evil magicians do exist, but they're rare. Why? Perhaps it's because they find simpler, surer ways to do their dirty work. It's far easier to beat up your enemy, sleep with his wife or her husband, rob them, or practice blackmail than it is to perform destructive magic.

Practitioners of negative magic burn themselves out. As we've seen, the projection of personal energy in magic is an expenditure of the life-force within. Once a magician has wreaked metaphysical havoc, there's no turning back—the current is closed. In programming personal energy with negativity, the magician infuses her/himself with negative power by unlocking it within, which paves the way for a life of darkness and, eventually, an early grave. Evil magicians destroy themselves with their own curses.

The vast majority of folk magicians, however, work with positive, healing, loving energies. They do so because:

Magicians respect life. All living creatures, including humans and animals, are manifestations of the universal power. As such, they're respected and loved, not cursed out of existence.

Magicians respect the Earth. Long revered in religions throughout history, the Earth is respected as the most intense manifestation of divine energy within our reach. It is also a source of incredible power. Therefore, magicians walk lightly upon the Earth and do nothing to upset its intricate balance, such as maliciously ending a life or cursing a human being.

Magicians respect the power. As the ultimate, universal force, the power is inconceivable. The energy that created galaxies, DNA, humans, and billions of forms of terrestrial plants and insects isn't something to challenge. It's even more unwise to misuse the power. Most folk magicians aren't afraid of the power; they wisely respect it.

Reverence of this energy is the basis of all religions. It is that which has been called God, Yemaya, Goddess, Kwan Yin, Grandfather, and every other human conception of the divine.

Power sent will be received in like kind. Performing negative or destructive magic ensures that such energies will be returned to the magician. Healing, peace, and prosperity are far more pleasant energies to receive. Some magicians accept the concept of the "law of three," which states that magical actions are returned in triple strength to the power-wielder. Performing a ritual intended to harm another person—even if it isn't effective—may bring death to the magician.

Magic is love. It is a loving movement of energy from one or more natural sources to effect positive, healing changes. For magic to be effective, the magician must have love for the self, love for others, and love for the Earth. Without these feelings magic stagnates and festers, turning into a brew of destructive energy which ultimately destroys the magician.

Heavy, isn't it? Yet it's so simple. Magic isn't hatred; magic is love. If we love ourselves we're willing to improve our lives. If we love others we're willing to help them find love, health, and happiness. If we love the Earth we're willing to work toward healing it of the ravages that one hundred years of "progress" has created.

Folk magicians harm none. They don't work magic to change other people's lives, even in seemingly positive ways, without first receiving permission to do so. Healing rituals aren't attempted without the consent of the sick. Folk magicians won't weave an aura of love-attracting vibrations around a lonely person without first asking.

To those who've been reared on the idea that magic is the ultimate weapon against humanity, these truths may be boring—but the truth often is.

While wide-eyed audiences watch curses and death-spells flying across flickering screens or running along the pages of cheap books, folk magicians continue to happily spread love, health, prosperity, peace, and security in their own lives and in those who've come to them.

They do this because they accept the basic rule of magic—

Harm none.

5

Other Forms Of Magic

Many forms of magic exist today, and folk magic is but one of them. The other two major types—*ceremonial* and *religious*—fall outside our definition of Witchcraft. However, because they're usually lumped in with all other occult practices under this heading, a brief look at them should serve to clear up some misconceptions.

Ceremonial Magic

Ceremonial (or ritual) magic is a contemporary system built upon both ancient and fairly recent traditions. It is based on Sumerian, Egyptian, Indian, and Semitic magic, with influences of Arabic, and later, Christian thought. Freemasonry also contributed to its present structure, as did the secret societies that were popular in Great Britain and throughout Europe in the eighteenth and nineteenth centuries.

Contrary to popular opinion, ceremonial magicians aren't concerned with conjuring up demons and stealing magical rings from monstrous, fly-headed spirits. They don't own flying carpets or take up residence in caves, and they certainly don't merrily plunge swords into unwilling victims or have imps as companions. Most importantly, they don't have any connections with Witchcraft, save in the minds of outsiders.

The ritual structures, terminology, and goals of ceremonial magic are usually—but not always—centered upon union with the divine, with perfection, and the expansion of consciousness. Or, as it is commonly described, "knowledge of and conversation with the magician's holy guardian angel."

That's a lofty spiritual goal, isn't it? This points out one of the key differences between ceremonial magic and folk magic. Unlike the latter, ritual magicians aren't usually concerned with the aims of folk magic: love, healing, money, happiness, and protection. When these needs are addressed through ceremonial magic (such as the creation of a talisman), it is usually as a means to an end—the attainment of the union mentioned above. In contrast, folk magicians solve problems in their lives with rituals, and rarely look further.

Some ceremonial magicians are organized into groups called *lodges* or *orders* (such as the famous Golden Dawn), and draw upon ancient Egyptian religion when devising their magical workings. Many of the rituals used by a splinter group of this magical lodge of the late 1800s have been published in *The Golden Dawn* by Israel Regardie, one of the most influential magical books ever printed (see Bibliography).

Other magicians attune themselves with more orthodox religions. The classical grimoires, or magical workbooks, of the Middle Ages and the Renaissance include invocations to Jehovah, Adonai, and God, and they utilize extensive Judeo-Christian terminology. This isn't heresy or mockery, but the product of a different interpretation of the Christian mythos. This is obviously far removed from folk magic, in which the power is sent forth without invocation to Deity.

Ceremonial magicians tend to be quite individualistic. Many practice their arts alone, spending long nights reading ancient texts, preparing their "tools of the art," and learning Latin and Greek to better perform their rituals.

Ceremonial magicians study the works of Aleister Crowley, along with those of William Gray, John Dee, Franz Bardon, Agrippa, Dion Fortune, and several other authors. Some delve into alchemy, geomancy, Enochian magic, and other subjects as sidelines or as the main course of their studies.

Ceremonial magicians are simply human beings who are not only working with energy (i.e., performing magic), but are searching for something greater that they have been unable to find in orthodox religions. They have a long, colorful history behind them filled with fantastic stories and exotic rites.

But they aren't Witches.

Religious Magic

Religious magic is that which is performed in the name of, or with the assistance of, Deity. It has been practiced by peoples all over the world, at all times in history, and it still has a vigorous following.

In earlier ages deities representing the fields, the mountains, springs, and woods were invoked during magic. The Moon and Sun were thought of as deities (or symbols of them), and were called upon during magical ritual. This was perhaps the purest form of religious magic.

Prayer is the quintessential example. When an individual fervently prays for a healing, a caring husband, or a studious daughter, the devout person directs personal power through the prayer and out to Deity. The person's emotional involvement in the prayer "programs" the energy being sent forth. The hoped-for result is, of course, a manifestation of the blessing being prayed for.

Unless the person praying is trained in magic, she or he isn't consciously aware that this process is at work. But this is unimportant. Prayers offered by devout persons of any religion are often answered. These prayers are effective because their personal energy, attuned with their magical need, is released toward Deity, and empowered by this larger energy source, manifests in Earthly form. The person's emotional state and belief in the Deity determines the effectiveness of the prayer.

Sacrilege? No. Just explanation.

Religious magic isn't practiced solely by lowly adherents to a religion. Priests, ministers, and others also perform it, and magic is an integral part of many current religions, including Christianity.

Specifically, divine power—that which has no physical form—is brought down to Earth through the agency of a priest or minister and is made to enter into certain objects. This form of religious magic includes the creation of, and use of, blessed religious medallions, crucifixes, and palm leaves worn by some Catholics for special favors. It is also the rationale of transubstantiation.

Other less ritualistic Christian sects utilize prayer and music to whip up a veritable brew of personal power to attune with that of the divine. Operators of revival meetings and charismatic Christian preachers know these secrets well, and effectively use them to elevate the consciousness of their followers to a high spiritual state.

But some individual believers—even Christians— have long brought elements of folk magic into their religion and have created a new form, one incorporating religious symbolism with the practices of folk magic.

This began once Christianity had established itself throughout Europe. Whether the new religious magic was an attempt to avoid persecution or death by outwardly converting to the new faith, or was a result of its practitioners' true conversion is open to speculation. But throughout the Middle Ages and Renaissance, an entirely new form of magic was practiced by the high as well as the low. It also marked the temporary abandonment of folk magic.

At one time, a woman wishing to prepare an herbal charm to protect her child would collect herbs while chanting ancient words, calling upon goddesses of healing and urging the plant to make its sacrifice for the benefit of the child. She'd fasten the herbs in cloth and hang this charm around her or his neck.

After Christianity's rise to power, the herbs were plucked with prayers to Jesus, God, or the Virgin Mary. Saints were often invoked (at least by Catholics). The cloth may have been stitched with a cross, symbol of the new religion that was often considered to have magical powers (witness its supposed effects on vampires). Finally, the magic charm was taken to a church to be blessed.

An extreme example of the people's belief in the powers of the church is the common medieval practice of stealing hosts from Catholic churches for use in protection spells, healing rituals and the like. *This was done not by Witches but by persons who had forgotten folk magic and had turned to the new faith. Witches had their own magic.*

Such a practice, which instilled horror among the religion's power-wielders, wasn't a mockery of Christianity or Catholicism. On the contrary, it was an acknowledgement of the power of the religion and of its priests, for only a true Christian could see power within a consecrated host or a piece of bread.

Many forms of religious magic are still present. Lighting a candle to a deity and asking for a favor is another form of religious magic, like any other type performed with supplications or invocations to higher powers, such as in modern Wiccan magic.

Naturally, religious magic is frowned upon by the religious officials; most deem it improper that humans should practice magic. It's seen as a move by the faithful to bypass human representatives of God and go straight to the source.

The Vatican can't be too happy about the fact that many Mexican-Americans wear medals depicting the saints for magical purposes, but this hasn't stopped the practice. Rituals involving ancient African deities are performed on the steps of churches in Haiti, Detroit, and New Orleans. Images of saints sit side by side with those of Chango and Yemaya on tens of thousands of household altars in the U. S. and Latin America.

Religious magic of this kind is common in the United States: the Bible is used to divine the future; crosses are viewed as protective amulets; psalms are recited to bring love, health, and happiness; images of Jesus, Mary, and St. Christopher adorn dashboards in cars. A thousand and one spells of this sort are used daily by persons of orthodox faiths.

Any form of folk magic can be performed by ceremonial magicians or within religious contexts. When this is done it ceases to be folk magic.

Be aware that the practices outlined in this chapter aren't those of folk magicians or Witches. They don't use Christian symbols in their rituals because thousands of others are available. They don't steal from churches because they don't believe in those doctrines. They also, generally, don't pray to Egyptian goddesses or Greek gods. Though they may be aware of the spiritual nature of the energy used in folk magic, they usually don't worship it in structured ritual forms. Wiccans certainly do, but folk magicians don't.

Folk magicians *work* with the powers of nature to improve their lives and the lives of friends and loved ones. Religious persons *revere* these energies, and prayer is often the only magical ritual which they practice.

6

Simple Folk Magic Rituals

The human experience is filled with numerous trials. Everyone has problems with money, love, health, and protection. Few of us haven't had times when we've nearly lost hope of ever getting out of the holes that we've dug for ourselves.

Some people give up. Some people pray for answers or miracles. And some, sadly, decide that this world isn't for them any longer and end their lives. Others, however, find a method of taking control of their lives.

As we've seen, folk magic is the movement of natural energies to bring about needed change. It is a means by which we can take control of ourselves and our lives, thus turning negatives into positives. It allows us to transform poverty into prosperity, sickness into health, loneliness into love, danger into security.

Though this isn't a primer of folk magic (see the

Bibliography for some suggestions), a few simple rituals are certainly warranted here. Such rituals can be performed by anyone who has a problem and wishes to correct it—not through supernatural forces but with the use of natural, *real* energies. Those who would never think of performing such rites can simply read them, and in doing so, learn something more about the ways and methods of folk magic. One of the techniques of demystifying a subject is to reveal it.

The following sections discuss two common problems of everyday life: love and money. Simple rituals are also given to solve these problems. These aren't ancient spells but they will work if carefully performed.

Just as a compact disc player set on "scramble" will replay the same songs for eternity unless this command is altered, so too must we change ourselves to accept the new energies aroused during magic. This change always starts within the mind. Make this change (as suggested in the discussions below), and the folk magic has a greater chance of being effective. Refusing to make the change is tantamount to asking for failure.

No unusual ingredients are needed for these simple rituals—no unicorn horns or rare plants. Only such basic items as candles, flowers, a mirror and coins are required. The rest is up to you. If you don't feel the need or desire to practice folk magic, fine. You'll know if the time comes.

Folk magic is an exciting tool of self-change. It is the birthright of every human being. It is a means of communicating with our deepest selves and with our planet—a tool that we can grasp and use to shape our lives into uplifting, immensely satisfying experiences.

Love

It's truly sad to think of how many people are desperately seeking love—usually in all the wrong places. They'll look for it in the eyes of strangers and at bars and parties; they'll search it out on sidewalks and in the frozen foods section of grocery stores. Thoughts of love may consume their entire lives at the expense of everything else. When they do find it, love is all too fleeting—an intimate dinner, a few nights of erotic heat, a series of phone calls and lunches. Then, just as they feared, the end. Their world is crushed. They can't go on without love. So they renew their search, knowing that somewhere they'll find their ideal mate.

Love is a drug.

We must make changes within ourselves to find love. If we don't love ourselves we certainly can't expect others to do so. If we don't have our own lives together we can't bring someone else into them. If we have nothing to offer another person why should they bother to offer themselves to us?

Psychology? Sure. Thought is a form of power. Our lives are pools of energy. By changing our thoughts we change our lives, creating new energy patterns, attracting other needed energies.

If we program our lives with love, love will be returned to us. If we put our affairs in order and take an active interest in our lives, they will run more smoothly. If we cultivate interests—those unconcerned with love or our jobs—we become richer persons with much more to offer to others.

This is a simple technique. Live your life fully in whatever manner is within your means and interests. Discover yourself so that you can share this with others. Continue to meet new people of both sexes. Keep looking, of course, but know that you can wait until the right person comes along.

In the meantime, perform this spell whenever you see fit. When you feel yourself starting to fall back into your old love-obsessive attitude, work this magic. When you ache and pine for past relationships, work this magic. When you feel you can't go on for another day without a love in your life, work this magic.

Then let it work its magic on you.

Petals Of Love

Only two magical tools are required for this ritual: a small mirror and fresh flowers. They can be daisies, carnations, violets, lilacs, or gardenias, but roses of any color are best. If you do use roses, remove the thorns from one of the stems.

Buy or collect seven or eight stems of the chosen flower. If cutting them yourself, thank the plant for its sacrifice in any words or actions that you see fit. Remember—nature is a power source. Magicians respect it.

Perform this ritual when you are quite alone and won't be interrupted. Take the phone off the hook, don't answer the door—give this time to yourself.

You may be dressed in normal clothes, those you sleep in or nothing at all. Do whatever feels most natural.

Place the flowers in a large vase or bowl. Nearby place a small mirror in a position so that you can see your face within it. Sit or kneel comfortably before the flowers. Remove one flower from the vase. Stroke it over your head, your hair, your ears. Move it up and down your cheeks and chin. As you do this, open yourself to the loving energies the flower is radiating out to you.

Close your eyes and brush their lids lightly with the flower. Say these words:

> *I see love.*

Move the flower lower. Smell its rich scent. Drink in its aroma. Let it fill your soul. Say:

> *I breathe love.*

Open your eyes. Move the flower away from your head and above it. Say:

> *I hold love.*

Lower the flower to your heart area. Stroke it up and down, soothing it, letting its energies melt into yours. Say:

> *I feel love.*

Move it down to your stomach. Press it gently against your skin or clothing. Say:

> *I nourish love.*

Still holding the flower in your hand before you, gaze at your reflection in the mirror. Say these or similar words:

> *Love is before me.*
> *Love is behind me.*
> *Love is beside me.*
> *Love is above me.*
> *Love is below me.*
> *Love is within me.*

> *Love flows from me.*
> *Love comes to me.*
> *I am loved.*

Place the flowers in a spot where you'll see them several times a day. If possible, wear or carry the flower you've used in your ritual. When it begins to wilt, bury it in the Earth, thanking it for its energies.

And be prepared to *receive* as well as to give love.

Money And Prosperity

In bygone times physical objects of genuine worth were used as money: precious gems, an ingot of pure copper, a gold bar, a silver dollar. In today's world, money is usually artificial. Governments print pictures and numerals on pieces of paper. We all agree that paper money is worth specific amounts and can be traded for hard physical goods and services. Similarly, virtually worthless metals are covered with thin films of copper and silver, and then stamped with more numbers and pictures. Some countries even mint aluminum coins.

If we've agreed that these bits of paper represent $10 or $100, then it must be apparent that money is a state of mind. A being alien to our planet faced with $10,000,000 in U.S. currency wouldn't see the wealth, but simply etchings and meaningless symbols.

This is important—wealth and prosperity are states of mind. All the money spells in the world won't bring us more wealth until we've learned to stop fearing money and its attendant responsibilities.

So before trying the following ritual, change your mind about money. If you truly need money, try to *want* it as well. If you simply want money, see how you genuinely *need* it too, how it can help improve your life and those of your loved ones.

Accept money into your life even before you have it. Ready yourself to receive it. Welcome it with open arms. Then begin.

A Silver Spell

This ritual takes a week to perform.

Situate a small bowl of any material in a place of prominence in your home, somewhere you pass by every day. Each day for seven days put one dime in the bowl.

Next, obtain a green candle. This can be any shade of green. Buy it at a candle shop, an occult supply store, a hardware store, or a supermarket. It can be a votive, a taper, or a columnar candle.

Before you begin, fix in your mind the idea that you are a prosperous person. See money as being no problem. Imagine money coming to you as you need it.

Place the bowl of dimes, the green candle, and a holder on a flat surface. Hold the candle in your hands and feel the power of money. Feel the avenues that open to you when you have it. Sense the energy within money which we as human beings have given to it. Place the candle in the holder. Pour the seven dimes into your left hand (or right if left-handed). You will create a circle surrounding the candle with the dimes. Place the first dime directly before the candle. As you place it say the following or similar words:

> *Money flow,*
> *Money shine;*
> *Money grow,*
> *Money's mine.*

Repeat this six more times until you've created a circle around the candle with seven gleaming dimes.

As you say the words and place the dimes, know that you're not just reciting and fooling around with pieces of metal. You're working with *power*—that which we've given money as well as that which is within yourself. Words too have energy, as does the breath on which they ride.

When you've completed this, light the candle. Don't just flick a Bic lighter; strike a match and touch its tip to the wick. As it picks up the fire, sputters, melts, and rises to a shining flame, see money energy burning there. See the power of money flowing out from the seven dimes up to the candle's flame and then out to the atmosphere.

Blow out the match, discard it in a heat-proof container, and settle down before the glowing candle and money. Sense the feeling of money in your life. Visualize (see with your mind's eye) a life with money to spare—a life in which bills are quickly paid and money will never again be a problem.

See yourself wisely spending money, investing it for your future needs. See money as an unavoidable and beautiful aspect of your life.

Kill off any thoughts of debt, of taxes, of doubts that you can achieve this change. Simply see what will be.

After ten minutes or so, leave the area. Let the candle burn itself out in the holder (don't use a wooden one). Afterward, collect the dimes, place them back in the bowl, and "feed" it a few coins every day from then on.

Money will come to you.

§

PART II

WICCA

§

7

The Religion Of Wicca

The people come together on a wooded hill beside the Missouri river. Stars wink and glow around the Full Moon high above the circling trees. Within the ancient oaks, fireflies buzz and flash their eerie light. The night air is still, hushed.

Forty people surround a blazing fire, hands linked, their attention directed toward the woman who stands before the blaze. Outlined by the leaping flames she begins an invocation to the Goddess.

The words, soft at first and then stronger, clearer, spill from her lips. "Goddess of the Moon," she says, "You of all power; we gather here on this night of the Full Moon in Your honor."

Twigs snap in the fire.

"God of the Sun, magnificent One, You of all power . . . "

The invocation ends. The woman raises her hands to the sky as the group begins moving clockwise with a slow step.

The people—some in hooded robes, some in street clothing—quicken their steps. They chant in a low monotone, their words unintelligible at first.

Wood crackles. Moonlight spills down. Naked feet kick through the dirt. Fast. Faster. The group practically flies around the blaze and the woman standing amidst them, as they turn their minds to their purpose.

After an unmeasureable time, the lone woman calls a halt. The group instantly stops, and its members simultaneously point their hands at the hooded figure. She glows, radiates, trembles, and directs the energy they've projected to her up to the Goddess, represented by the glowing orb in the sky.

Exhausted, the group sits on the bare Earth. Watching the fire, they talk and laugh and pass around wine and crescent-shaped pastries.

Their rite has ended.

Folk magic is but half of what is termed Witchcraft. The other half is the religion known as Wicca. There are at least five major ways in which Wicca differs from other religions. These are:

- Worship of the Goddess and God
- Reverence for the Earth
- Acceptance of magic
- Acceptance of reincarnation
- Lack of proselytizing activities

Wiccans revere the *Goddess and God.* Current Western religion, Wiccas feel, is out of balance. Deity is usually referred to as God (as opposed to Goddess). God the Father is a common term. The concept of male "saviors" directly descended from male divinities is widespread, even outside of Christianity. The representatives of these organizations—such as religious officials, priests and ministers—are usually male, though this is slowly changing. To sum up, contemporary Western religion focuses much of its attention on *maleness.*

The Wiccans are different. They see nature as a manifestation of the divine. Because of this they argue that a male divinity revered without a female deity is, at best, only half effective. Both sexes exist in nature. If nature is a manifestation of divinity, then divinity also manifests in male and female forms. Hence modern Wicca is usually (but not always) centered around reverence of the Goddess and God. *Both*—not one, not the other.

Such a concept, though it may seem surprising in today's world, is certainly not new. Ancient religions are replete with deities of both sexes. Faiths in many parts of the world today are also in line with this concept. Where ancient religions live unhindered by well-meaning but culture-destroying missionaries, goddesses and gods are still worshipped as they have been for millenia.

So Wicca is a religion built around worship of these two deities, the Goddess and the God. They are often thought to be twin energies, or nonphysical manifestations of the power that was discussed during Part I of this book.

As primeval peoples began practicing folk magic, some sensed presences or personalities within the forces of nature. This was the advent of all religion.

Wicca is in harmony with ancient religious practices and principles. It isn't a step backward, for Wicca has been structured to speak to these times. Nor is it a slap in the face of Christianity or any other contemporary, male-based religion. Wicca is an alternative religion, one that is fulfilling to its adherents.

The Earth is revered by Wiccans as a manifestation of the Goddess and God, and nature signifies the processes and wonders of the Earth that are undetermined by humans. Because nature and our planet are linked to the Goddess and God, they are both sacred, holy.

The Earth is a living organism, a direct gift from the Deities. Other religions preach that the Earth is a world of illusion; an arena upon which to store up credits that will be cashed in after death, or simply a tool that humans can, and should, "dominate and subdue." Wiccans, in contrast, respect the Earth.

Many Wiccans belong to ecological organizations or groups dedicated to halting the senseless slaughter of animals for human beautification. They may protest nuclear reactors, which have the real potential for causing far greater harm than good. They fight developers who bulldoze trees and cover acres of land with concrete and blacktop.

Because they see the Earth as a manifestation of the Goddess and God, Wiccans are concerned about its welfare: they lend it human energy in order to help it recover from the ravages which humanity has inflicted upon it. In this sense, Wicca is truly an Earth-religion.

Magic, as we've seen, plays some role in most religions. In Wicca it's given a more prominent place. Wicca isn't religious magic, though its followers certainly do practice it. It isn't a magical religion, either.

Wicca is a religion that embraces magic, that welcomes it as an opportunity to attune with divine, Earthly, and human energies.

Because Wicca is truly a religion, magic takes a secondary role in its rituals. Even if a rite is performed for a specific magical end, the Goddess and God are always invoked before the power is sent.

The magical aspects of Wicca confuse outsiders, perhaps because in most other religions only priests or saviors are believed to be able to, in a word, channel divine energies. Wicca isn't so exclusive; it views magic as a natural part of life and of religion.

Reincarnation is an ancient teaching that most Wiccans acknowledge as reality. Basically, reincarnation is the doctrine of rebirth—the phenomenon of repeated incarnations in human form to allow for evolution of the sexless, ageless human soul.

While reincarnation isn't an exclusive Wiccan concept, it is happily embraced by most Wiccans because it answers many questions about daily life and offers explanations for more mystical phenomena such as death, birth and karma.

Some say "Reincarnation? Bah! That's just Eastern stuff!" It's true that reincarnation is best known from teachings that originated in what we now know as India. However, the idea itself is probably as old as human existence.

A seed drops onto the Earth. It sprouts and bursts into life. Leaves unfurl. Shoots rise up and explode into flowers. Seeds drop to the ground. The plant withers and dies, but by next spring another plant will struggle up from the soil.

The doctrine of reincarnation may have originated

from observation of natural processes such as this. Those who have accepted it as reality, including many Wiccans, have found it to be comforting.

The fifth major difference between Wicca and most other religions is that it is *nonproselytizing*. No person is ever pressured into becoming Wiccan. There are no threats of eternal hellfire and damnation, no retribution for not practicing Wicca. The Goddess and God aren't jealous deities, and Wiccans aren't frightened or subdued by them. Candidates for initiation (of which more will be said in Chapter Nine) don't denounce their former faiths. Wicca is not a brainwashing, human-controlling cult masquerading as a religion.

Wiccas don't recruit new members, then smack their lips and rub their hands together as more enter the religion. There are no Wiccan missionaries, no "witnesses," no Wiccan press-gangs.

This may seem surprising to those raised in orthodox religious frameworks, but it is based on a sound, true concept which is the antithesis of most other religions' teachings:

No One Religion Is Right For Everyone

Perhaps it's not too strong to say that the highest form of human vanity is to assume that your religion is the only way to Deity—that everyone will find it as fulfilling as you do, and that those with different beliefs are deluded, misled, or ignorant.

It's understandable why most religions and their followers feel this way, and why they participate in converting the masses. Watching others change to their faith reestablishes that faith's genuineness in the mind of the converter. Some members of orthodox religions are truly concerned for the souls of non-believers, but this is based on their religion's narrow-minded teachings.

Another aspect of proselytization involves politics. If Religion *A* converts Country *B*, it increases its political and financial power in that country. The same is true of important persons. Orthodox religions have far-reaching influence in the realms of government and finance. Political candidates backed by major religions are often elected, and then propose or support legisla-tion that furthers that religion's interest. This may all be on the sly (voters may not know the true nature or extent of the candidate's links with organized religion) but the effects are the same.

Money is also a powerful incentive to spread the word. Organized religions today in the United States take in billions of tax-free dollars every month. True, some of this money is spent on charitable causes, but the bulk of it pours right back into the faith's bureau-cracy, fattening the bank accounts of the individuals who run it. So the more followers, the more money.

Wicca simply isn't like this. It isn't organized to this extent. National groups do exist, but mainly for social and sometimes legal reasons. Regional gatherings of Wiccans may draw hundreds of persons, but local covens usually number less than ten members, and many Wiccans practice their religion alone, with no group affiliation.

Wicca isn't a financial institution and doesn't strive to become one. Students don't pay for initiation. Small fees, where they do exist, are similar to dues required in any group to pay for supplies, refreshments and so on.

So the stories of Wiccans (read Witches) belonging to a worldwide organization that aims to rule the world are false. So too are the lies about Wiccans trying to coerce others into joining their religion. They simply aren't that insecure.

Don't worry; Wiccans aren't out roaming the streets plotting to force little Jimmy to join a coven, or to bilk Aunt Sarah out of her life's savings.

They're content to practice their religion in their own way—either alone or with a few others. They are aware of the differences between Wicca and other religions, as well as of the ultimate goal of all: union with Deity.

8

The Goddess And The God:
The Divine Aspects Of Wicca

When I was in the fifth or sixth grade I read a book
about Greek and Roman religion. After describing
ancient rituals devoted to the likes of Diana, Pan,
Demeter, Zeus, and Proserpina, the author stated
something to the effect of: "Of course, no one wor-
ships these gods today."

Even that early in my life I remember asking myself
"Why not?"

Many others have felt the same way. Male-dom-
inated, monotheistic religion has had to make room
for the mushrooming interest in Wicca and other
polytheistic religions. Tens of thousands of persons
from all walks of life are attuning with deities associated with the Earth, the Sun and Moon, the sea, and
the winds.

Many of these persons come to Wicca, and in
doing so, find a religion that speaks to them. Because
Wicca *is* a religion, the Goddess and God are all-

important. The rituals, symbols, tools, chants, and dances serve to celebrate the Deities in specifically Wiccan ways, and magic is used to create a common ground where humans enhance their relationships with divinity. However, a personal relationship with the Goddess and God is what Wicca is all about.

The mention of the religious aspects of Wicca may prompt some questions. Who are these mythic figures? What are their names, their attributes, their stories? How can Wiccans attune so closely with deities scarcely acknowledged, or completely ignored, by the outside world?

Such questions are difficult to answer in all but the most general ways, for the religious experience is one shared with Deity alone. No two Wiccans can describe the Goddess in exactly the same way, just as no two Christian descriptions of God would be the same.

The Deities are known by countless names, most of them drawn from ancient religions—British, Egyptian, Greek, and Roman names are frequently used.

Just as Isis grew from a localized deity worshipped in a small area of ancient Egypt to a nationalistic Goddess ruling everything from childbirth and healing to beer-making and navigation, so too do the Goddess and God claim dominion over a vast number of natural phenomena.

This chapter explores some facets of the Goddess and God as they are known to some Wiccans. This is the heart and soul of the religion.

Lady Of The Moon; Earth Mother; Sister of Power

The Goddess speaks:

I am the Great Mother, worshipped by all creation and existent prior to their consciousness. I am the primal female force, boundless and eternal.

I am the chaste Goddess of the Moon, the Lady of all magic. The winds and moving leaves sing My name. I wear the crescent Moon upon My brow and My feet rest among the starry heavens. I am a field untouched by the plow. Rejoice in Me and know the fullness of youth.

I am the blessed Mother, the gracious Lady of the harvest. I am clothed with the deep, cool wonder of the Earth and the gold of the fields heavy with grain. By Me the tides of the Earth are ruled; all things come to fruition according to My season. I am refuge and healing. I am the life-giving Mother, wondrously fertile.

Worship Me as the Crone, tender of the unbroken cycle of death and rebirth. I am the wheel, the shadow of the Moon. I rule the tides of women and men and give release and renewal to weary souls. Though the darkness of death is My domain, the joy of birth is My gift.

I am the Goddess of the Moon, the Earth, the Seas. My names and strengths

are manifold. I pour forth magic and power,
peace and wisdom. I am the eternal Maiden,
Mother of all, and Crone of darkness, and I
send you My blessings of limitless love.*

The Goddess is the female force, that portion of
the ultimate energy source which created the universe.
She is all-woman, all-fertility, all-love.

In Wicca She is perhaps most closely associated
with the Moon. Not that Wiccans *worship* the Moon.
They simply see it as a celestial symbol of the power,
both manifest and unmanifest, of the Goddess. Some
Wiccans call the Goddess Diana in Her lunar aspect.
Most meet for worship on the nights of the Full Moon
each month.

She is also associated with the Earth. The entire
planet is a manifestation of Goddess energy, a tangible example of the powers of Mother Nature. Wiccans may revere Her in this aspect as Gaea, Demeter,
Astarte, Kore, and by many other names.

The Goddess is inextricably linked with women in
general. Childbirth, menstruation, and other women's
mysteries were anciently celebrated with religious
rituals. Many feminist Wiccan groups today still perform such rites.

Indeed, the rebirth of Goddess worship in general
in the last few years has had a dramatic influence:
western women, who have long been denied access to
the feminine aspect of Deity (save in the thinly dis-
guised Mary worship in the Catholic Church), have
found their voices and themselves within the Goddess.

---

* Based on an invocation written by my first Wiccan teacher and included in
Wicca: A Guide For The Solitary Practitioner.

Many are heavily involved in politics in an effort to secure women's well-deserved equality in society. Others are active in antinuclear campaigns. Some are so Goddess-oriented that they don't invoke the God in their rituals. This is the result of thousands of years of male-oriented religion. Feminist Wiccan groups devoted solely to the Goddess, once viewed as upstart and nontraditional (i.e., nonvalid) by some more traditional Wiccans, have settled into their own space and are now a growing and influential movement within Wicca. They're certainly fulfilling a need for women to rediscover the Goddess within.

Perhaps most Wiccans know the Goddess in three aspects, corresponding to the three stages of life. These are the Maiden, the Mother, and the Crone. The declaration of the Goddess that preceded these words amply examined these stages.

The triple aspects also relate to the phases of the Moon. The Maiden corresponds to the New and waxing Moon, the Mother to the Full, and the Crone (also called the Hag or Wise Grandmother) to the waning Moon.

Wiccans see the Goddess at work in their daily lives. The birth of a new idea may show Her hand. Flowers bursting into full glory are seen as manifestations of Mother Earth's abundance. The initiatory processes of pregnancy and birth are also linked with the Goddess.

Just as members of conventional religions establish personal relationships with their conceptions of Deity, so too do Wiccans with the Goddess. She is everywhere, all around them—in the Earth, the Moon, and within themselves.

The Horned One; The Harvest King

The God speaks:

I am the radiant King of the Heavens, flooding the Earth with warmth and encouraging the hidden seed of creation to burst forth into manifestation. I lift My shining spear to light the lives of all beings and daily pour forth My gold upon the Earth, putting to flight the powers of darkness.

I am the master of the beasts wild and free. I run with the swift stag and soar as a sacred falcon against the shimmering sky. The ancient woods and wild places emanate my powers and the birds of the air sing of My sanctity.

I am also the last harvest, offering up My grain and fruits beneath the sickle of time so that all may be nourished. For without planting there can be no harvest; without winter no spring.

Worship Me as the thousand-named Sun of creation, the spirit of the horned stag in the wild, the endless harvest. See in the yearly cycle of festivals My birth, death and rebirth—and know that such is the destiny of all creation.

I am the spark of life, the radiant Sun, the giver of peace and rest, and I send My rays of blessings to warm the hearts and strengthen the minds of all.

The God is the male force, the other half of the primal divine energy acknowledged by Wiccans. He is all-man, all-fertility, all-love.

Wiccans see the God represented by the Sun. In earlier times, before the tilt of the Earth's axis was known to be the cause, the changing seasons were thought to be created by the varying warmth of the Sun. Though Wiccans are well aware of current astronomical knowledge, they still see the Sun, and therefore the God, as being linked with the coming of spring, summer, fall, and winter.

Wiccans celebrate the changing of the seasons with specific rituals (See Chapter 13). These "days of power" or Sabbats occur eight times a year. They mark the seasons and the changing fertility and weather patterns of the Earth. Though the Sun and the God is still (*symbolically*) viewed as the originator of these changes, both deities are revered at these times. Many Wiccans identify food with the God. Food is a product of the Goddess' fertility and of Her union with the God. Thus He is both parent and child.

Harvest, then, which traditionally coincides with the coming of fall, is a time of the God's sacrifice "upon the sickle of time," as I expressed it in the above passage. It is marked with Wiccan rituals to the Goddess and the God.

The Wicca also see the God in the wildwood, in its ancient trees, tangled vegetation, and undomesticated animals. In particular, horned animals such as the stag and the bull are thought to be linked with the God. Horns were ancient symbols of divinity, so the God is sometimes referred to as the Horned One. (This is *not* a reference to Satan, no matter how much some outsiders wish it to be.)

Some Wiccans place the role of death upon the God, perhaps because of His symbolic transition every autumn. As the God brings death, the Goddess, source of all nourishment and fertility, brings life anew through the phenomenon of reincarnation.

To Wiccans, the concept of the God isn't something brushed off only upon ritual occasions. He is, with the Goddess, a part of their lives every morning, noon, and night.

Though some Wiccans dedicate themselves and their rituals solely to the Goddess, most revere Them together. They view nature and the Earth, even our own bodies, as manifestations of the interplay of Their energies.

In Wiccan thought, the Goddess and the God are the twin divine beings: balanced, equal expressions of the ultimate source of all. This unknowable, incomprehensible source is that which has been revered within all religions since the beginning of spiritual thought and practice.

To clear up the major misconception regarding Wiccan ("Witch") deities, a few words are certainly appropriate here.

Wiccans don't worship the Devil. This amazingly common falsehood (that Wiccans are Devil-worshipers) is vigorously promoted by television evangelists, and would be absurd if it hadn't caused so much bloodshed.

Wiccans aren't Devil-worshipers. They aren't Satanists. They aren't anti-Christian or pro-Christian. In common with hundreds of millions of other human beings, Wiccans simply *aren't* Christian. They aren't crazed individuals attacking other religions, nor are they backsliding Christians eager to worship their particular concept of evil.

As discussed in this chapter, Wiccans revere the Goddess and the God. Outsiders—those with something to gain—can, and certainly do, interpret this on their own terms: "Gee, they don't worship The One True God. They're Satanists!"

This same thinking led earlier Christians to believe that unconverted Africans, Europeans, native American peoples, Polynesians, Australian Aborigines, and many other cultural groups were card-carrying Devil-worshipers. Because they weren't Christian and had different customs, they weren't human. This fostered wholesale slaughter and the unimaginable concept of slavery.

Such a narrow-minded viewpoint is still alive among less aware Christians. I've already discussed the pitfall of assuming that your religion is the only genuine method of contacting Deity, so I won't reiterate it here but will mention it again to explain why Wiccans and Witches are thought to be Satanists.

They aren't. They're simply members of a different religion.

Many, many humans have found comfort in attuning with their conception of the divine. So too have many Wiccans.

All religions have one ideal at their core: to unite their followers with Deity. Wicca is no different.

9

Initiation

There are many ways to become a Wiccan. None of them, despite outsider's lies, involve the renunciation of the candidate's former religion.

In the recent past Wicca was primarily a secret, initiatory religion. In this "traditional" Wicca, most practitioners were members of covens (see Chapter 10). Covens are small groups of Wiccans who meet for study, worship, and magic. Some of these covens were primarily training organizations with varying memberships. As candidates learned the basics of ritual craft, they moved on and newcomers took their places. Others, however, retained cohesive group identities and rarely allowed new members to join.

This is still true today, but many nontraditional covens now exist. Some are noninitiatory, arguing that human beings really have no right to initiate others. Others are self-initiatory, viewing this process as the domain of the Goddess and God.

Initiation is an age-old practice. It usually consists of a ritual that demonstrates and celebrates the acceptance of an individual to a group, religion, or a specific level of society. Confirmation and first communion serve as two examples of Christian initiation. Anthropological textbooks, as well as back issues of *National Geographic*, discuss rituals in which young adults are subjected to circumcision, tooth extraction, scarification, and other drastic rites of passage.

Initiations aren't always performed as religious events. In American corporate society the presentation of the key to the executive rest room is a form of initiation. Hazing rituals of various degrees of danger are commonplace among college sororities and fraternities, and graduation day at military boot camps marks the conclusion of a long initiatory process designed to transform a civilian into a member of the armed forces. Initiation ceremonies among such groups as the Shriners, Masons, Boy Scouts, and Girl Scouts are well known.

In Wicca, though, initiation is a mystical process. Traditional initiation rituals are usually dramatic experiences designed to awaken within the candidate a new consciousness that is attuned with the Goddess and God.

If the ceremony is properly enacted, the person undergoing the ritual is profoundly changed. She or he certainly emerges from it with a new identity as a Wiccan, and perhaps acquires a magical name; but the intent of the process is to expand her or his awareness of alternate states of consciousness and nonphysical realities.

Some covens perform initiations routinely, without

a genuine sense of the ceremony's goals. Others view it with what I feel is the proper respect, for it is a ritual which changes the person undergoing it in many subtle and obvious ways.

Just what does a traditional Wiccan initiation ritual consist of? It can be broken down into five major stages:

A *purification* of some kind is usually undertaken. Among some groups this may be no more than a week or so of daily meditations, or a dip in an herbal bath and anointment with scented oils. In others, a strict dietary regime is presented to the candidate a week before the ceremony itself. The diet may eliminate meat, sugar, caffeine, alcohol, and other foods—all of which are thought to reduce psychic awareness. The use of illicit drugs is prohibited by virtually all Wiccan groups, so the breaking of such addictions may also be a part of purification. Some Wiccan groups use the notorious symbolic scourging as part of the purification process—as well as the "ordeal" (see below).

A *challenge* of some kind is often presented to the candidate. This usually consists of questions: are you prepared? Do you wish to enter the religion of Wicca? What can you offer the Goddess and God?

Next, the candidate may undergo some type of *ordeal*. In some groups this consists of a symbolic scourging as mentioned above. The use of the scourge in Wicca—even in a symbolic sense—has caused much controversy and muckraking. It isn't used by all Wiccan covens, or even by the majority of them. Where it is used it's used in a symbolic sense, and ties in with one of the major Wiccan myths: The Journey of the Descent of the Goddess into the Underworld (printed

in full in *The Meaning of Witchcraft*—see Bibliography).
It is performed without inflicting physical pain.

A *symbolic death and rebirth* usually follows. This is a
worldwide feature of initiations, signifying the "death"
of the candidate's earlier life and a rebirth into the
religion or group. It may consist of simply being given
a new magical name.

Or the candidate may be wound around with black
cloth to symbolize a fetal state within the Goddess in
Her mother aspect. The cloth is slowly unraveled and
she or he emerges as a Wiccan person.

Following this, a *dedication* often occurs in which
the new Wiccan offers testimony of her or his dedication to the Goddess and God through words, gestures, or deeds.

The candidate is now a member of Wicca, and
usually, a member of a coven.

That's about it. No pacts with the Devil, no human
sacrifices, no disturbed graves or demonic rites. Just a
simple, dramatic ritual that serves to bring an outsider
into the religion.

Until recently, this was the only way to become a
member of Wicca. Exclusivity was the norm; if you
weren't initiated by an acknowledged member of an
acknowledged Wiccan tradition (see Chapter 10) you
weren't, in some eyes, a true Wiccan.

This is changing. Self-initiation is a phenomenon
of our times. Many are frustrated by fruitless searches
for covens and qualified teachers. Thus, a woman in
Kentucky may walk out under the Full Moon, spill
wine upon the bare earth and dedicate herself to the
Goddess. Or a man may lie on a grass-covered hill
with his arms and legs outstretched so that his body

forms the shape of the pentagram (a five-pointed star). In a moment out of time, the primal energies of the Earth and Sun surge through him and he discovers the presence of the Goddess and God within.

As early as 1970, initiated Wiccans were writing articles wondering if such persons were *really* Wiccans. The answer lies not within human minds or opinions but within the realm of spirituality, within the Goddess and God Themselves.

After all, Wicca and all religions serve one major purpose: to facilitate communication with Deity. If self-dedicated Wiccans establish relationships with the Goddess and God, observe Wiccan holidays, use Wiccan tools and uphold Wiccan ideals, what initiate can dare state that they aren't Wiccan?

Self-dedicated Wiccans are, truly, Wiccans as much as are those who have undergone initiation into the religion (and to a coven) at the hands of another human being.

In truth, the initiatory process doesn't consist of a physical rite. That is the outer form only. True Wiccan initiation is a process by which a human being becomes increasingly aware of the presence of divinity within, of those strong spiritual connections with the Goddess and God. This may take place instantaneously, but it is usually a gradual transformation.

Initiation may outwardly manifest in a love for nature and for the Earth. The person may have the urge to join ecological or animal-protection societies. A change in diet—even to the extent of embracing vegetarianism—may also manifest.

In quiet moments she or he may hear the music of the Moon as it rises and sets, and the glow of power from the Sun. The stars may cease to hold mysteries and may instead promise answers.

The endless cycle of seasons, the intricate processes of nature, and the planet upon which we live may be revealed as blessed manifestations of the Goddess and God.

Even the physical body—the flesh and blood and bone—is newly seen as a storehouse of ancient memories and a magical power generator.

When this and much more that can never be put down into words occurs within an individual, no physical rite of passage is necessary unless desired by the individual. She or he has experienced the ultimate Wiccan initiation—by and within the Goddess and God.

10

Wiccan Traditions

A tradition is a specific method of action, attitude, or craft that has been handed down from one generation to another. Among Wiccans, however, the word has a slightly different meaning. To them tradition signifies a specific set of rituals, ethics, and tools. In short, a Wiccan tradition is a specific Wiccan subgroup.

This chapter will explore the different kinds of Wiccan traditions. Because none of them are truly dominant (indeed, many Wiccans now proclaim no allegiance or lineage to any), we'll be looking at the differences between specific Wiccan traditions, as opposed to examining any one of them. This avoids the possibility of stepping on toes and revealing "secrets."

"Hi. What's your tradition?"

This question was once quite common wherever Wiccans met. The answer given often determined the bulk of the questioner's opinion concerning the answerer. Such sectarianism is melting away in the umbra of the 1990s, but it is still alive among more narrow-minded members of the Craft, as Wicca is also called.

A Wiccan tradition is a specific, structured system within the larger framework of Wicca. Unlike the widely divergent viewpoints to be found within Christianity, most Wiccan sects agree on the five basic points of the religion mentioned in Chapter 7:

1. The Goddess and God are acknowledged through timely rituals linked to the Moon and Sun.
2. The Earth is revered as a manifestation of divine energy.
3. Magic is viewed as a natural and joyous part of the religion and is used for life-affirming purposes.
4. Reincarnation is accepted as fact.
5. Proselytizing activities are taboo.

Not all traditions agree in whole with these five points. Many others would add several more. And indeed, one of the major divisions within Wicca is the prominence of the Goddess in worship. As mentioned previously, some Wiccans (whether affiliated with a tradition or not) devote their religious and magical activities exclusively to the Goddess. For others, the balance of *both* the Goddess and God is seen to be the ideal for religious workings.

I can't think of any Wiccan tradition that wouldn't agree with points 2 and 3, though they may have different teachings concerning these aspects of their religion.

Point 4, reincarnation, is again generally accepted.

But here again wide latitude exists. Some traditions insist that the human soul always incarnates in the same sex: i.e., if you're female in this life, then you always were and always will be female. Others see this aspect as far less structured. Few if any accept the belief that humans incarnated as molds, flowers, insects, or animals before "evolving up" to the point at which they could inhabit human bodies.

Point 5 is universally recognized.

Even allowing for such minor variances, most Wiccan traditions accept these five points. These five principles, along with a small-group structure and the tools utilized in ritual, are what makes Wicca Wiccan.

What, then, are the differences between individual Wiccan traditions? Here are some specific areas:

The Name. The name of the tradition in which they were initiated used to be of great importance to many Wiccans, for it signified the shape of their ritual workings, their world view, and their ideas concerning the Goddess and God.

For example, Georgian Wiccans utilize different ceremonies than, say, the Dianic Feminist Wicce. Their ideas concerning the nature of Deity may be radically different as well.

Many traditions have been named after either their earthly founder or the individual most closely associated with it. One excellent example of this is Gardnerian Wicca, named by nonmembers after Gerald Gardner. (Books detailing specific traditions can be found in the Bibliography.)

In the late 1960s and early 1970s exclusivity was all the rage. An initiate of Tradition A might not have recognized initiates of Tradition B as true Wiccans.

This is understandable, as the same has occurred among sects of most major religions.

But the time when the name of one's tradition was so important is over. Many Wiccans—even those initiated into rigid traditions—have assumed nonsectarian viewpoints. They welcome all other Wiccans into their rituals and confidences without prejudice, or in the words of one tradition, with "perfect love and perfect trust."

Ritual system. Among many traditions, the specific rituals actually used by members—religious as well as magical—are secrets that the initiate cannot reveal. This, then, is at the heart of the tradition. Rituals are skeletons, or patterns, for movement and speech. Their structure and the words, music or dance used—even the time at which they are performed—vary from tradition to tradition. This is in part because each group identifies with slightly different concepts of the Goddess and God. Because rituals serve to unite humans with Deity, rituals performed for specific Deity-concepts differ from those of others.

A Seax ritual is thus far different in particularities than one of, say, the Gardnerians. This doesn't imply that one is better than the other; only that different human beings have different needs.

Remember, the only legitimate reason for practicing a religious ritual of any kind is to attune with Deity.

Wiccan traditions keep their particular rituals in what is often called the "Book of Shadows." These are rituals which utilize that specific tradition's nomenclature and tools, and which serve to distinguish one tradition from another.

In Wiccan traditions, magical rituals are group workings designed to rouse, program, release, and project natural energy to achieve personal or group goals. As such, these rites are usually more closely guarded than religious ceremonies. And because they're often done in connection with religious workings, they, too, reflect that tradition's specific mindset.

Ritual practices. Some Wiccan traditions perform their rituals at night; others prefer the day. Some gather together and worship the Goddess and God in street clothing. Others prefer robes, and still others wear nothing at all (see Chapter 15.) To make things even more complicated, initiates of some traditions shroud their heads with hoods during ritual; others don't use them.

Many traditions stress outdoor rituals, while others never leave the living room. Most traditions allow women and men to participate in their rituals and to gain entrance to their system; others admit only women, and a few, only men. Many attempt to achieve a balance of women and men within each coven.

Every tradition has definite reasons for holding on to their particular ritual practices, and it certainly isn't anyone else's business how one tradition's members achieve union with the Goddess and God and practice magic.

Covens. Covens, which can be narrowly defined as groups of Wiccans initiated into a single tradition to practice Wicca, are the keepers of each tradition. But even here there are plenty of options. Some covens maintain 12 or 13 members; others have anywhere up to 50 (known as a "college"). In some, only two or three members are necessary to form a coven.

Some traditions allow, and even encourage, initiates to practice alone; others practically forbid it, deeming coven membership to be necessary to Wiccan practice within their tradition.

Coven hierarchy. This has been a hotly debated point among Wiccans. Some traditions continue the practice of providing three separate initiations for members. These have different names among various traditions. Some call them "levels," as in "Level 1." Others simply term them First Degree, Second Degree, etc. They may be symbolized by animals that have specific divine or totemic aspects within the tradition. Certain symbols are used within some traditions to designate each "degree" (this term is Masonic).

The basic form of the first of these three initiation ceremonies was described in Chapter Nine. It is an entrance to the religion of Wicca, to the specific tradition, and to the coven.

The second initiation usually takes place after religious and magical training within the tradition. This is known as Second Degree, or the second level. In some traditions a Second Degree Wiccan may be known as a "lesser priestess," or "lesser priest." Second Degree acknowledges much training within the tradition and mastery of Wiccan principles.

The Third Degree creates what are commonly known as "High Priestesses" and "High Priests." This has been described as the pinnacle of achievement within a specific tradition. It takes place, in theory, only after completion of a rigorous training program encompassing magic, structure of ritual, magical group dynamics, Wiccan mythology, and a number of other areas, depending on the particular tradition.

Among hierarchal covens, only Third Degrees may lead the rituals and run working covens. Thus covens in these traditions are led by:

A High Priestess
or
A High Priestess and a High Priest.

A High Priest alone rarely runs a coven.

During rituals the High Priestess (HPS) may act as the representative of the Goddess, the High Priest as the God. The HPS may draw the Goddess into herself and act as Her representative. In a sense, this practice is a form of religious Wiccan "channeling," but it isn't widespread among Wiccan groups.

Having said all that, many traditions don't use such a system of initiatory degrees. Covens may be run by one, two, or three persons, who may be elected by other members. Learned and experienced Wiccans are certainly respected, but they aren't necessarily in charge. Coven leadership may also change at each ritual.

Confusing? It's just another indication that Wicca is very much a religion of individualism.

Tools. As we'll see in Chapter 11, specific physical objects are used in Wiccan rituals for a variety of religious and magical purposes. Though some tools are standard among most traditions (such as the *athame*), some are not. A tradition's use or non-use of a tool again illustrates the independence that exists between Wiccan groups.

So these are a few of the areas in which Wiccan traditions differ from one another. This lack of cohesion is one of the strengths of Wicca, for the seeker can usually find an appropriate path among the various traditions.

For further, in-depth information regarding specific Wiccan traditions, consult the Bibliography.

11

Ritual Tools

"The *cauldron* is ringed with flowers . . . "
"Point the *athame* skyward and project
   energy . . . "
"Float a flower in the water-filled *cup* and
   scry the future . . . "

Cauldrons, athames, and cups—these are a few of
the tools that Wiccans use in their religious and magical rituals.

Some of these may appear to be ordinary household objects, and indeed they can be. Few houses lack
brooms or knives. Large, round-bottomed cast iron
pots are still to be seen on dusty shelves or in cob-
webbed attics. And cups of every shape and variety
are used in daily life by billions of human beings.

Yet Wiccans see these as more than sweeping
tools, cutting implements, or drinking vessels; they

see these things as religious objects—not to be venerated, but to be used in ritual to attune themselves with the Goddess and God.

Wiccan tools may be forged in full sunlight, carved at the rise of the Moon on the Summer Solstice, or purified with basil leaves in a forest clearing. Wiccans are encouraged to make their own tools if possible. Those that lay outside the range of their talents are traded or purchased outright, and indeed, it can be a trial to obtain a full set of Wiccan tools. However they may be obtained, Wiccan tools are usually reserved solely for ritual workings.

Most of the tools described here aren't used in any other religion. Where they are used, it's often for very different purposes. This chapter discusses the majority of Wiccan ritual implements, but again, it is a generalized list drawn from a number of different Wiccan traditions.

Images Of The Goddess And God: Aphrodite standing on a seashell rising from the sea. Diana (in alabaster) with Her bow and hounds. A celestial Goddess with a crescent Moon upon her brow, hands spread, hair flowing around her head. A reproduction of one of the famous "Venus" statuettes of prehistoric cave-dwelling times.

Herne the Hunter. Jack of the Woods or The Green Man, with oak leaves curling around His face and trailing out from His mouth. Pan with His pipes. A satyr. A horned God stalking the woods, bearded and muscular. Osiris in all His ancient, solar glory.

Many Wiccans use images of the Goddess and God in their rituals. This is all that they are—images. Pictures. Three-dimensional representations which remind practitioners of Their presence.

Wiccans don't worship such images. They aren't viewed as being the abodes of the Goddess and God; Wiccans aren't that idiotic. These are only pictures, just as a photograph isn't the person depicted within it but merely a representation of her or him.

Wiccans bristle when they're accused of being "idol-worshipers" by outsiders. They aren't idolaters any more than are Catholics who wear crucifixes, or Christians who hang pictures of Jesus on their walls.

Images of the Goddess and God are just that. They may be carved out of stone or wood, or cast in metal. Artistic Wiccans fashion their own images, and others obtain them from statuary stores or occult houses.

But many Wiccans don't utilize such defined images, viewing them as being too limiting. They may prefer to use abstract representations: a stone egg, a round stone, or a round mirror to represent the Goddess; an acorn, pine cone, or arrow-shaped stone to represent the God. Some simply use two candles to represent Her and Him.

The *athame*, or ritual knife, is usually a black-handled knife with a steel blade that may be double- or single-edged. The athame (it has other names but this is the most common) is never used for cutting purposes. It certainly isn't used for living sacrifices of any kind, despite lies to the contrary. In fact, the athame is an instrument of magic and power. It is utilized to direct natural energy from within the body to the outside world. Though systems differ, the athame is seen to be sacred to the God in some traditions.

A sword, which is simply a longer version of the athame, may be used in its place but is generally limited to coven workings.

The *white-handled knife* is used in Wiccan and magical ritual for practical purposes such as cutting herbs or piercing a pomegranate, as opposed to the purely symbolic use of the athame. It is never used to perform living sacrifices.

The *cauldron* is a large metal vessel, usually made of iron. Ideally, it stands on three legs and has an opening narrower than its widest part.

The cauldron, which is firmly linked in popular imagination with Witches, is a symbol of the Goddess and all that She encompasses—the universe, completion, reincarnation, fertility, abundance, and love. As such, energy generated during Wiccan magical workings may be directed into it.

Fires may be lit within the cauldron for ritual purposes. It may be circled with flowers, or filled with water and used to divine the future. Despite popular misconception, brews are rarely created in the cauldron, and when they are, no lizard's legs or other oddments are thrown into it—just leaves and herbs and water.

The *wand* is much like those used by early ceremonial magicians. It is often fashioned of wood, and may be engraved with symbols or studded with stones. Some are made of silver and quartz crystal.

The wand is an instrument of invocation. It may be held and raised while speaking words of invitation to the Goddess and God during a Wiccan ritual. Unlike the athame, it is rarely used to direct energy.

The *pentacle* is a flat piece of metal, clay, wood, stone, or some other natural substance on which various symbols are engraved or carved. One of these symbols is the pentagram, the five-pointed star used in ancient magic.

Contrary to what televangelists and radical Christians have been saying, Wiccans don't use the pentagram to represent Satan. Perhaps Christians do, but Wiccans certainly don't. Outsiders can believe whatever they wish—and they do—but they should look at their own religion. At least one church in Europe (in Germany, I seem to remember) has large stained-glass pentagram windows. This points to the antiquity of the symbol and its usage among many religions.

The pentacle sometimes acts as a base upon which other tools or objects are placed while being charged with energy during rituals. It is symbolic of the Earth and abundance.

The *cup*, or chalice, is another Goddess symbol and is simply a cauldron on a stem. It may contain wine or water, which is ritually imbibed. This isn't a parody of Christianity. The cup has as much—or as little—connection with the chalice used in holy communion as does the cauldron.

The *censer*, or incense burner. In common with many ancient and contemporary religions, Wiccans smolder incense in honor of the Goddess and God and also to prepare the working area for ritual. It also acts to shift awareness to the spiritual world behind the physical, and it needs no hallucinogenic ingredients to effect this change.

Bowls of salt and water are frequently used as well. Mixed together, these two substances form a purifying liquid which may be sprinkled around the ritual area before religious and magical workings. Salt and water may also be sprinkled separately; traditions differ.

Cords of various natural materials and colors are also used in Wiccan magic rituals among certain traditions. Though symbolism varies, cords usually signify the material world and manifestation of magical goals. They're also symbolic of the bond of love between coven members, and of that between the Wiccan and the Goddess and God.

The *broom* is sometimes used in ritual. It may be lightly brushed around the working area to purify it as an alternative, or in addition to, the use of salt and water. The broom is seen as a symbol of both the Goddess and the God, and is of ancient religious usage.

Fresh flowers or greens may be present to lend their traditional energies to the rite or spell at hand. They also represent the vegetative deities and the fruitfulness of the Earth.

Bells and musical instruments may be used during Wiccan rituals to mark specific parts of the workings or to shift consciousness. Bells were once used to drive off evil, a custom echoed in the familiar church bells. The bell is sacred to the Goddess in Wiccan symbolism.

The *labrys* is a two-headed ceremonial axe once utilized in ancient Cretan rituals. It may be used by Wiccans to represent the Goddess or for symbolic magical acts, but never to chop or cut anything— particularly humans or animals.

Other tools may include the *scourge*, used in some Wiccan traditions for, once again, symbolic scourging during initiation and other ceremonies; the *staff*, a large form of the wand (or the broom without the bristles) used for hiking to remote ritual areas through

rough terrain, or to draw the physical representation of the "magic circle" (see Chapter 12) on the ground; and many others.

The bulk of these tools are used in ritual for various purposes, among these being:

• To create the area of worship. Since Wiccans rarely have buildings set aside solely for ritual workings (indeed, this isn't even considered to be ideal), sacred space is created at each ritual (see Chapter 12). The athame and sometimes the wand are used for this purpose. The salt and water as well as the broom may also be used to purify the area. The censer is also at work here, for its smoke creates the appropriate atmosphere through scent.

• To invoke the presence of the Goddess and God during ritual. The wand is the primary tool used here. However, most Wiccans agree that the Goddess and God are within us as well as outside of us. This tool— and Wiccan ritual—is a method of contacting that part of us linked with the divine. The Goddess and God aren't called as if They were pets.

• To serve as focal points for power during magic. An object can be placed upon the pentacle. Some groups use the cauldron.

• To direct energy toward its destination. The athame is the most widely used tool of energy direction, though a pointed finger will also serve this purpose. A few Wiccan traditions use the wand, but this is rare.

Wiccans realize that the tools themselves have no power save that which they give to them. In fact, most Wiccans agree that the tools aren't really necessary, but that they do enrich ritual practices.

Some Wiccans won't allow others to handle their tools. They're thought of as being personal objects. Tools may be kept in storage (wrapped in silk, for example), and taken out only for specific use.

Others share tools among themselves—borrowing athames for ritual, loaning out an extra cauldron to a new Wiccan. Some constantly utilize their tools, believing that the more they work with them, the more effective they will be in their hands and with their energy.

So these are some of the tools of the religious and magical workings of Wiccans. They aren't demonic. They aren't weapons or instruments of evil. They aren't used to stab, hurt, or kill anyone or anything. They are, quite simply, objects that some humans have found to assist them in linking in with Deity.

In this light they are truly sacred.

12

Circles And Altars

The circle is a unique geometric figure. It is without beginning and without end—a symbol of perfection. It defines space efficiently, without sharp angles or corners. It contains and also resists intruding forces or energies.

Stand in the center of a flat, treeless plain. Look up at the horizon and spin slowly around. The bowl of the sky seems to be a circle above your head.

At the full of the Moon, when the orb rises just at sunset, it shows itself as a round globe of glowing white light. The Sun, too, appears as a flat circle when it sinks in the west.

Though we can't know for sure, these may have been some of the reasons that ancient peoples utilized circles in magical workings. They were seen as protective devices as well as representations of the Sun and Moon, and thus, as the spiritual essence of our physical environment—Deity incarnate.

Most magical textbooks (see Bibliography) contain intricate instructions for creating a "magic circle." Throughout the Middle Ages and Renaissance periods, this was the magician's most powerful tool against the spirits that were invoked. The magician stood inside this circle and conjured the spirit to visible appearance within a triangle placed nearby (but outside) of it. In this case the circle was used for its protective quality.

Wiccans don't raise spirits or demons, but they do utilize circles. The first Wiccan books, beginning in 1954, made much of the magic circle. In this creation of psychic energy, the Wiccans met with the Goddess and God and performed rituals of worship and magic.

It wasn't until fairly recently that the true nature of the circle was publicly revealed. It isn't a circle but rather a *sphere* of energy. The Wiccan projects energy from the body through the athame. With visualization she or he fashions this energy into a sphere of glowing light.

Half of this sphere is above the ground, the other half is below. Thus, the magic circle represents the place where this sphere cuts into the ground.

A circle defines space in two dimensions, a sphere in three. Thus in Wiccan thought, the sphere is an ideal sacred space for ritual.

This may be confusing to outsiders. Why don't Wiccans just build temples of stone, brick, and masonry and get on with it? Some do, but even then the sphere is still created prior to most rituals.

The reasons for this are simple:

- The magic sphere (circle) creates a place often described as being "between the worlds"—a common ground wherein humans can communicate with the Goddess and God.

- The creation of the magic circle is one of the key rites of Wicca, one that differentiates it from other religions.

- Magically constructed temples of this nature are preferred to physically constructed places of worship.

Therefore, Wiccans truly have no temples built of human hands. Yes, they may set up working quarters in a room, a barn, or an outbuilding, but even these aren't genuine temples. The Wiccan temple is a transitory construction, built and dismantled with each and every ritual.

Think about this for a moment. If a member of an orthodox religion were to physically build his or her church before every session of worship, wouldn't it be that much more effective in performing its task?

Materially minded humans construct impressive edifices, carefully designed to induce spirituality within the believer. Wiccans create temporary temples of magical energy. Thus it is this energy—its quality and effects on the human psyche—which creates the proper mood within the Wiccan. I've termed this "ritual consciousness."

Wiccans fashion circles (remember, this is a misnomer; these are actually spheres of energy) wherever and whenever needed. They may be created in apartment buildings; on beaches and prairies; high on mountain tops; within automobiles; or while walking down lonely, dangerous streets. Wiccan circles have been successfully made in hospital rooms to speed the healing of recovering patients.

The physical surroundings aren't important so long as they're conducive to concentration and attention to the magical work at hand, for making a circle is indeed an act of Wiccan magic.

It precedes nearly every rite. If indoors, the area is cleansed and purified using some of the tools mentioned in Chapter 11. After this, the altar is arranged with the tools necessary for the ritual, and the sphere of energy is created around it. Religious or magical workings may then begin.

This isn't mysterious, though it may seem to be to nonpractitioners. The circle is a powerful construction of energy, though. Within a magic circle the sensitive can truly feel that she or he is apart from the everyday world, in a realm of magic, energy, and spirituality.

The altar usually sits within the center of the circle. This may be a table, a rock, a tree stump, or even a cleared area of ground during outdoor rites. Its basic function is to hold the tools used during the ritual.

Although this is an introductory book, it seems best to include a complete Wiccan ritual to show, exactly, one method of how a magic circle is formed.

This was once a closely guarded secret, but many books have been published revealing its exact construction. So it seems that a work of this type wouldn't be complete without a specific example.

The following ritual, into which I've inserted notes in parentheses where needed, isn't ancient but it is fairly representative. I wrote it for inclusion in the book *Wicca: A Guide For The Solitary Practitioner*, published by Llewellyn.

A bit of explanation is necessary before we begin.

This circle-casting is drawn from a tradition I wrote named "The Standing Stones Tradition." Since I wrote this purely for publication in the above mentioned book, it isn't a "living" tradition. Nonetheless, I hope the ritual below will clear up some questions regarding what is perhaps the central Wiccan ritual.

Here it is, in full:

The Circle Of Stones

The Circle of Stones is used during indoor rituals, for energy raising, meditation and so on.

First, cleanse the area with the ritual broom.

For this circle you will need four large flat stones. If you have none, candles can be used to mark the four cardinal points of the circle. White or purple candles can be used, as can colors related to each direction— green for North, yellow for East, red for South, and blue for West. (Different traditions relate the colors and directions in other ways. This is one system.)

Place the first stone (or candle) to the North, to represent the Spirit of the North stone. When in ritual you invoke the Spirits of the Stones, you're actually invoking all that resides in that particular direction, including the elemental energies. (No, Wiccans don't invoke spirits; the term "spirit" is used here because it's less sexist than the more usual terms "King" or "Lord." The five elemental energies mentioned are: Earth [related to the North], Air [the East], Fire [the South], Water [the West], and Akasha [omnipresent on the Earth]. The first four are emanations of the fifth.)

After setting the first stone (or candle) to the North, place the East, South, and West stones. They should mark out a rough square, nearly encompassing the working area. This square represents the physical plane on which we exist: the Earth.

Now take a long purple or white cord (fashioned, perhaps, of braided yarn) and lay it out in a circle, using the four stones or candles to guide you. It takes a bit of practice to do this smoothly. The cord should be placed so that the stones remain *inside* the circle. Now you have a square and a circle, the circle representing the spiritual reality. As such, this is a squared circle— the place of interpenetration of the physical and spiritual realms.

The size of the circle can be anywhere from five to 20 feet, depending on the room and your desires.

Next, set up the altar. The following tools are recommended:

> A Goddess symbol (candle, holed stone, statue)
> A God symbol (candle, horn, acorn, statue)
> Athame
> Wand
> Censer (as well as incense)
> Pentacle
> A bowl of water (spring, rain, or tap)
> A bowl of salt (it can also be placed on the pentacle)
> Flowers and greens
> One red candle in holder (if not using point candles)
> Any other tools or materials required for the ritual, spell, or magical working

Set up the altar according to your own design. Also, be sure to have plenty of matches, as well as a small heat-proof container in which to place them when used. A charcoal block is also necessary to burn the incense (unless you're using stick or cone incense).

Light the candles. Set the incense smoking. Lift the knife and touch its blade to the water, saying:

> *I consecrate and cleanse this water*
> *that it may be purified and fit to*
> *dwell within the sacred Circle of Stones.*
> *In the name of the Mother Goddess and the*
>   *Father God*
> *I consecrate this water.*

(I purposefully left out specific names for the Goddess and God in this ritual, and throughout the book, to allow the interested student to discover with which deity-forms she or he feels most comfortable. And again, deity names can be seen as limitations. Some Wiccans don't use them at all.)

As you do this, visualize your athame blasting away all negativity from the water.

The salt is next touched with the point of the knife while saying:

> *I bless this salt that it may be fit*
> *to dwell within the sacred Circle of Stones.*
> *In the name of the Mother Goddess and the*
>   *Father God*
> *I bless this salt.*

(Salt is blessed rather than purified because it is considered to be pure.)

Now stand facing North, at the edge of the cord-marked circle. (The Wiccan now summons up personal power from within her or his body, readying it to be projected during the circle-casting.)

Hold your athame point outward at waist level. Walk slowly around the circle's perimeter clockwise, your feet just inside the cord, charging the area with your words and energy.

Create the circle through your visualization, with the power flowing out from your knife's blade. As you walk, stretch the energy out until it forms a complete sphere around the working area—half above the ground, half below. As you do this say:

> *Here is the boundary of the Circle of Stones.*
> *Naught but love shall enter in,*
> *Naught but love shall emerge from within.*
> *Charge this by Your powers, Old Ones!*

("Old Ones" is a poetic reference to the Goddess and the God. The last sentence calls upon the Goddess and God to charge, or empower, the circle and the rite which follows with their energy.)

When you have arrived back at the North, place the athame on the altar. Take up the salt and sprinkle it around the circle, beginning and ending in the North and moving clockwise. Next, carry the smoking censer around the circle, then around the Southern point candle or the lit red candle from the altar. Finally, sprinkle water around the circle. Do more than carrying and walking; sense these substances purifying the circle. The Circle of Stones is now sealed. (And cleansed and purified.)

Hold aloft the wand at the North, at the edge of the circle, and say:

O Spirit of the North Stone,
Ancient One of the Earth,
I call you to attend this circle.
Charge this by Your powers, Old Ones!

As you say this, visualize a greenish mist rising
and writhing in the Northern Quarter over the stone.
This is the elemental energy of Earth. When the Spirit
(i.e., the elemental energy of Earth associated with the
North. This is *not* a conjuration of a demon, but a sum-
moning of natural energy!) is present, lower the wand,
move to the East, raise it again and say:

O Spirit of the East Stone,
Ancient One of the Air,
I call you to attend this circle.
Charge this by Your powers, Old Ones!

Visualize the yellowish mist of Air energy. Lower
the wand, move to the South, and repeat the following
with your upraised wand, visualizing a crimson Fire
mist:

O Spirit of the South Stone,
Ancient One of Fire,
I call you to attend this circle.
Charge this by Your powers, Old Ones!

Finally, to the West, say with wand held aloft:

O Spirit of the West Stone,
Ancient One of Water,
I call you to attend this circle.
Charge this by Your powers, Old Ones!

Visualize the bluish mist, the essence of (the element of) Water.

The circle breathes and lives around you. The Spirits of the stones are present. Feel the energies. Visualize the circle glowing and growing in power. Stand still and sense it for a moment.

The Circle of Stones is complete. The Goddess and God may be called and magic wrought.

Releasing The Circle

(After Wiccan rituals it's customary to release or disperse the circle to return the area to normalcy. I've heard of few traditions that fail to do this.)

Once the rite is ended, face North, hold aloft the wand and say:

> *Farewell, Spirit of the North Stone.*
> *I give thanks for your presence here.*
> *Go in power.*

Repeat this same formula to the East, South, and West, substituting the proper direction in the words. Then return to the North and hold the wand aloft for a few moments.

Lay the wand on the altar. Take up the athame. Standing in the North, pierce the circle's wall with the blade at waist level. Move clockwise around the circle, visualizing its power being sucked back into the knife. Literally *pull* it back into the blade and handle. Sense the circle dissolving, shrinking—feel the outside world slowly regaining its dominance in the area.

When you arrive at the North again, the circle is no more.

That is one example of a Wiccan circle-casting.

Though it is written for a solitary practitioner most are designed for group workings, even though only one individual may be involved in the actual creation of the circle.

I can't state often enough that the "Spirits of the Stones" mentioned above aren't disembodied human souls—not ghosts or demons or imps. They're what some Wiccan traditions term the "Lords of the Watchtowers," or the "Queens and Kings of the Elements." These are elemental energies that are called to be in attendance during rituals for protective purposes, as well as to lend their special energies. This practice is nearly universal in Wicca.

In Wiccan thought the circle is deemed the most fit place to honor the Goddess and God, but it also has a second function: to contain and concentrate magical energy. This is a lesser function. Indeed, the circle isn't necessary for successful group or solitary magical workings.

In essence the magic circle is a nonphysical, yet real, temple in which humans—Wiccans—walk with the Goddess and God. As such it is one of the hallmarks of Wiccan practice, but it isn't absolutely necessary for group worship.

Wiccans may conduct simple rituals while out walking in lonely hills or sitting on the beach, gazing into the water. They may commune with the Goddess and God as the Sun rises or the Moon sets. A group of Wiccans on a picnic or a trip to the countryside may suddenly decide to perform some kind of ritual. Without tools they may simply sit or stand in a circle and perform their working.

During all but spontaneous rituals, however, the

magic circle is usually constructed, and it is within this sphere of energy that rites of worship and magic are performed.

The circle (sphere) of energy is the Wiccan temple.

13

Days Of Power:
Sabbats And Esbats

Christians celebrate Christmas, Easter, and a host of other holy days. Orthodox Jews acknowledge Hanukkah, Passover, and other times with specific rituals and customs. Here in the United States, we bring pine trees into our homes at the end of December, dye eggs in spring, and pass out candy to children on October 31st. And all over the world, peoples of various faiths observe days of the year with religious and secular rites.

All religions have sacred calendars containing various days of power, or times associated with particular deities. Wiccans are no different. Most perform religious rituals at least 21 times a year: 13 Full Moon celebrations, usually Goddess-oriented; and 8 Sabbats, or solar festivals, related to the God. Some Wiccans meet with their covens for these rites, while others perform them alone.

First we'll discuss the Full Moon rituals.

Esbats

The <u>Moon</u> is an ancient symbol of the Goddess. Countless religions have recognized it with rites and ceremonies. Contemporary Wiccans often gather (if coven members) on nights of the Full Moon every 28 days for worship and magical ritual.

This doesn't mean that they *worship* the Moon. Wiccans see in the Moon a symbol of the Goddess, not Her face. The Moon's dramatic cycle of waxing and waning long ago attracted religious awe from peoples attuned with nature. Wiccans may admire the Moon's beauty, and may thrill to seeing it slowly rise from the eastern horizon, but they don't worship it.

The Moon is also seen as a mystic source of energy. Wiccans know that though it glows at night, the Moon possesses no light of its own. It reflects light from the hidden Sun. Because light can be equated with power, and because of the Moon's strong, proven effects on the tides and the cycles of both women and animals, Wiccans draw energy from the Moon during Esbats to further empower magical workings.

Thus an Esbat (or, more commonly, a Full Moon Ritual) is a rite involving worship of the Goddess and a magical working. In every Wiccan tradition with which I'm familiar, the worship comes first—before the magic.

I have memories of past Esbats—of the Moon setting over the ocean, creating a shimmering, dazzling path of silver light on the water as we worked simple rites on the sand. I recall candle-lit rooms dense with incense smoke and moonbeams filtering in through opened windows. To Wiccans, the time of the Full Moon is a time of sanctity and spirituality.

The ritual usually occurs at night. The circle is cast, the Goddess (and the God) is called in poetic words, with mystic music or sacred dance. A meditation or psychic session may follow, after which works of magic are carried out beneath the light of the Moon.

Afterward, the coven or the solitary practitioner frequently sips white wine or fruit juice and eats crescent-shaped cakes.

This is the Esbat—a time of reverence and magic.

The Sabbat

Whereas Esbats are determined by the Moon, Sabbats recognize the shifting of the seasons. They're connected with old European planting and harvesting rites and ancient hunting ceremonies, as well as with the solstices and equinoxes.

These are sometimes known as "days of power," or "high days." And though daytime rituals would seem to be preferred for solar festivals, most Sabbats are held at night.

For covens these are times to gather and work their rites, a time to be reminded of the passing of the seasons and the changes at work within the Earth, which is especially important for city-dwellers. Again, Wiccans don't worship the Sun, but see it as a symbol of the God.

All religions have specific reasons for scheduling rituals. For Wiccans, the seasonal cycle determines the positioning of rituals.

In essence, the Sabbats tell a story of the God and the Goddess. In festival form they reveal a seasonal and agricultural Wiccan legend. Wiccan traditions vary a great deal in their myths. Much of this variance is due to the specific cultural context of the tradition, such as Celtic, Feminist, and so on. However, a generalization of the meanings of the eight Sabbats can be formed.

Many Wiccans begin their year with *Samhain* (October 31st). On this night they revere their friends and loved ones who have passed on to the other life. Because Wiccans accept the doctrine of reincarnation, this isn't a completely somber festival but a quiet recognition of the inevitable outcome of life. Many Wiccans also mark the symbolic death of the God on this night. Samhain is linked with the coming of winter and ancient hunting rituals.

This date will be recognized in the United States as Hallowe'en or Hallows Eve, a night on which adults and children dress in costume and attend parties, and newspapers blazon stories about Witches, curses, and ghosts across their pages. These are folk memories of the old European customs that were played out at this time of the year. Wiccans usually ignore such occurrences, for this is a sacred night.

Yule (*circa* December 21st; the exact dates of the Solstices and Equinoxes change every year) celebrates the rebirth of the God through the agency of the Goddess. Some might note the date and believe this to be a mockery of Christianity. Actually, that isn't quite the case.

Early Biblical scholars tried to place a date for the birth of Jesus. Coming up empty-handed, they adopted the Winter Solstice. This date was changed to December 25th so that it wouldn't vary from year to year. Yule was probably chosen for this purpose because it is an ancient Pagan religious day—Mithras, for example, was thought to have been born then. Early Christians were noted for superimposing their religious symbolism and theology onto that of earlier religions, thereby attempting to speed conversion.

So Wiccans celebrate Yule as the date of the rebirth of the God (symbolically seen as the Sun). The Winter Solstice marks the depths of winter. From this night on, the hours of daylight grow longer until midsummer.

Imbolc (February 1st or 2nd) is the time when Wiccans celebrate the recovery of the Goddess from giving birth to the God. It is a festival of purification and of reverence for the renewing fertility of the Earth. Bonfires may be lit.

Ostara (*circa* March 21st), the Spring Solstice, marks the first day of true spring. It is a time of the awakening of the Earth (the Goddess in her terrestrial aspect), as the Sun grows in warmth and power.

Pagan rituals of spring, such as coloring eggs, have survived to this time by being transferred to Easter celebrations.

April 30th is known as *Beltane*. At this festival the young God ventures into manhood. He and the Goddess (His mother/lover) join and produce the bounty of nature.

And before anyone thinks—aha! Their gods practice incest!—remember that this is nature symbolism. In Wiccan thought the Goddess and God are united, one—twin halves of a whole. They are dual reflections of the power behind the universe that can never be truly separated.

May Day is still a time of flowers, maypoles (once an openly sexual symbol), and chains of clover, even among those who don't practice Wicca.

Midsummer (*circa* June 21st) is the point at which the powers of nature (created by the union of the Sun and the Earth) are at their peak. Wiccans gather to celebrate and to practice magic. Huge bonfires may be lit in honor of the Sun. This night and its magic was honored in one of Shakespeare's plays.

Lughnasadh (August 1st) is the beginning of harvest. The God weakens as the first grains and fruits are cut. Lughnasadh is a ritual of Thanksgiving. Indeed, the American holiday of Thanksgiving is an echo of Pagan European harvest festivals. If the Pilgrims had planted their crops on time, Thanksgiving would more closely correspond to the date of Lughnasadh.

Mabon (*circa* September 21st) is the second harvest. The God prepares to leave His life behind Him as the last fruits are gathered to nourish the peoples of the Earth. The warmth is lessening day by day.

Samhain follows Mabon, and so the cycle of rituals is completed.

Remember, this is the barest outline of the Sabbats. Individual traditions possess rich lore concerning each day. Intricate, symbolic rituals are enacted on the Sabbats in honor of the God and Goddess, as reflected in seasonal changes.

Foods symbolic of each day are often placed on the altar and eaten during the sacred meal, sometimes known as "Cakes and Wine," which follows most Sabbats. Specific crafts may be worked which link with the symbolism.

Magical rituals may also take place, though many Wiccans reserve the Sabbats as times for worship only.

Samhain and Yule and all the others are, to Wiccans, what Christmas and Easter are to Christians.

They are holidays (holy days) that Wiccans set aside each year to commune with the Goddess and God.

The Sabbats and Esbats can be seen on three levels. First, they're times of religious worship in which Wiccans meet with the Goddess and God—times of renewing contacts with the Deities in a structured ritual setting.

Second, these days of power are also specific times for working magic to help, heal, comfort, and protect Wiccans and their friends and loved ones. This is done with the assistance of the Deities.

Finally, these are also celebrations—times for laughter, shop talk, and feasting. When the religious and magical workings (if any) are over, and after the circle has been dispersed, the Sabbats and Esbats become parties.

These Wiccan rituals aren't parodies of other religions' most sacred ceremonies. In fact, the Sabbats are rooted in the earliest expressions of religion among humans, which predate Christianity by thousands of years.

If anything, they're based on rites far older than those of any other religion.

14

Wiccan Magic

Wiccans, in common with folk magicians, rouse, program, release and direct personal power to manifest needed changes. In other words, they practice magic. Though Wiccan magic follows the same rationale as folk magic, the techniques used may be quite different.

Folk magicians burn candles, manipulate quartz crystals, or use herbs and oils and other tools to effect magical changes. Wiccan covens usually perform group-oriented rites involving the raising of energy, and they use few or no physical tools save for the most potent of all—the human body.

The magic outlined in this chapter primarily refers to that practiced by covens and groups of Wiccans. Solitary Wiccans may utilize similar rituals or practice folk magic while calling upon the Goddess and God to assist them.

The goals of Wiccan magic are often similar to those of the folk magicians. Healing is perhaps the most common objective. Wiccan magical goals may also be concerned with love, finances, employment, protection, and many other goals. And despite popular misconceptions, Wiccans don't curse or hex. It simply isn't practiced or taught.

Wiccan magic may also tackle larger problems, such as world peace. Many covens began working toward this goal in the late 1960s, when it was common for covens to literally join forces in sending energy to halt the Vietnam War.

Wiccans also work magic to arrest exploitation of the Earth, to conserve its natural resources, and to send energy back to our planet in order to ensure its continuing ability to maintain life.

Wiccan magic is also used to create the sphere of power (magic circle) in which rituals are performed, as well as to purify and charge tools used in religious and magical ceremonies.

Wiccan methods of raising energy were long kept secret, revealed only to coven members after initiation. Today, many of these have been openly published in one form or another. Some are peculiar to Wicca.

The most common form is known simply as the dance. Physical activity, as we've seen, generates personal power. Because the body is a storehouse of life-energy, muscular contraction produces power readily available for use in magic. Wiccans have long known this, and have used specific movements to build up energy during rites of magic.

After the religious rites have ended, the High Priestess, High Priest or some other coven leader discusses the goal of the magical rite to be performed by the group. In some covens each member works toward her or his own magical goal. Thus, eight or ten or thirteen Wiccans generate power simultaneously to send it toward their own personal needs. Most commonly, however, a group goal is utilized.

In any case, the desired outcome is clearly visualized in each Wiccan's mind. A symbol of it may be placed on the altar or written onto small pieces of paper, which are then burned. After this the magic begins.

The Wiccans join hands and move clockwise around the altar, maintaining the visualization. This is called the dance, simply because the coven circles the altar with linked hands—not because they're actually dancing to choreographed steps. During the Witch trials, many Witches were accused of performing the infamous "back-to-back" dances; however, these dances aren't performed.

The coven circles faster and faster until it becomes a blur to anyone who watches. During this time the Wiccans are steadily increasing their energy. At the appropriate time, when the coven's power has risen to its peak, the group leader signals the members to release their energy, and through visualization, send it toward the goal. In some groups each member projects personal power to the leader, who then directs the power outward to the Goddess and God or to its final destination.

After the dance, the magical rite is over. The Wiccans may feel temporarily exhausted, for this is an expenditure of power. But soon everyone returns to normal, often helped by a ritual meal.

If a folk magician can raise a sufficient amount of energy to effect magical changes, it follows that a group of persons working toward the same goal can produce a tremendous amount of power. Group magical workings, whether Wiccan or not, can be spectacularly effective.

Perhaps a few words should be said here concerning clockwise (*deosil*) movement. In Wicca, clockwise motion is thought to generate energy with positive qualities. Conversely, counter-clockwise (*widdershins*) motion draws energy with negative qualities. Some say this is simply symbolism, but others claim it to be more than this.

The term "clockwise" refers not to the motion of the hour, minute, and second hands of a modern dial clock, but recalls an earlier timekeeping device.

Sundials have been used for untold millenia. These consist of a base marked with numbers at appropriate angles around its rim. A thin shaft rises from the center of the sundial. As the Sun moves across the sky each day, this pointer's shadow moves in an arc from left to right, denoting the hour. Thus clockwise originally referred to the motion of this shadow.

Now, if the Sun casts a shadow in this way, and the Sun is related to all that is good and bright and nourishing on our planet, it follows that motions in the opposite direction are its antithesis.

Thus through the centuries, counterclockwise movements have been used in negative magical workings. This has been called the "left-hand path." Most Wiccans avoid widdershins movements during their rituals.

This is why the Wiccans dance around the altar in a clockwise direction. Some Wiccans south of the equator—particularly in Australia, which has a thriving Wiccan population—reverse these directions. That is, of course, their prerogative.

Back to Wiccan magic. The dance is but one form. There are others, but most are similar. In one, the coven is arranged in a circle around the altar. The members may stand still, link arms, and chant or hum, while visualizing the magical goal and raising personal energy. As before, the leader determines when the available power is at its greatest concentration, and again informs the coven to release its energy.

Or a symbol denoting the magical goal may be marked onto a piece of paper or wood and placed on the altar. Gathered around it, the coven raises personal energy, and through their athames, projects it into the symbol. This is finally burned or buried to release the power to go to work.

Other Wiccan groups utilize variations on the above forms—or may even practice a type of ceremonial magic to achieve their goals. No matter what type of coven magic is used, it is usually effective.

Folk magic, as we have seen, is governed by one basic dictum: harm none. As a religion embracing magic, Wicca follows the same rule, though it is often differently worded:

"An it harm none, do what you will."

(The *an* used here is an archaic form of *if*, not a variant of *and*.)

This phrase is almost universally known to English-speaking Wiccans. Its origins remain shadowy. Many feel that it was put into these words in the 1940s or 50s, and was based on the magical motto of ceremonial magician Aleister Crowley: "Do what thou wilt shall be the whole of the law. Love is the law; love under will."

While the origins of this phrase are misty, its message is quite clear. Wiccans don't practice negative magic. They don't break up marriages, force persons to fall in love, or harm others through their rituals. Sure, Wiccans get angry. They may get into fist fights or toss a drink in an obnoxious man's face. But they'd rather cut off their right arm before "hexing" or "cursing" another human being.

In the popular mind, magical power seems to be equated with the lack of morality. This is as absurd as thinking that the possession of a knife inclines its owner to stab everyone she or he meets. At best, true mastery of magical power only occurs within individuals who subscribe to "An it harm none, do what you will."

The possibility of misuse of Wiccan magical techniques was one of the rationales for secrecy in the past. "Don't reveal magical methods to the untrained," some Wiccans said. "They may misuse them." While there may have once been some logic behind this idea, it is no long valid. Wiccan magical techniques have been openly published. Anyone with ten dollars (or a library card) can read most of these "secrets."

I'm sure that there have been some groups who called themselves Wiccan and practiced negative magic. But to call these groups Wiccan or use them to judge the majority of Wiccans would be as incorrect as calling those unfortunate souls who perform satirical masses and desecrate the host "true Catholics"—or Wiccans.

Wiccan magic is performed for positive ends. It is engaged in for coven members, for friends and relatives, for the Earth, and for all its peoples. It is a positive, participatory aspect of the religion of Wicca.

15

Nudity, Sex, And Wicca

These are hot topics—in more ways than one. In the first draft of *The Truth About Witchcraft*, the booklet that preceded this work, I excluded the section on sex and Witchcraft. I added it to a later draft and it appeared on pages 21-22.

When it came time to write this book, I hesitated to include this chapter. I was unwilling to add fuel to the arguments of narrow-minded outsiders who gleefully claim that Wicca consists of nothing more than orgies. However, common sense told me that to ignore these aspects of Wicca might lead some to believe that nudity and sex are more prevalent within Wicca than is the case.

Hence this chapter.

Let's get right down to the point here: nudity doesn't always lead to sexual activity. And indeed, complete nudity isn't even necessary for sex (as evidenced by centuries of Asian erotic art). While the two can be, and certainly are, complementary to each other, doffing one's clothing isn't necessarily a prelude to sex.

The state in which I live, California, led the fight for legally recognized clothing-optional beaches in the early 1970s. Police reports show that the number of occurrences of sexual activity on the infamous Black's Beach (a once-legal nude recreation area) was actually *lower* than that of other conventional beaches. What does this seem to say?

Just this: that to persons who are comfortable with social nudity, who have no hang-ups regarding the naked human form, nudity is a truly social—not sexual—state.

What does this have to do with Wicca? One aspect of the religion that has been most attacked is the fairly common use of ritual nudity. That is, religious rituals performed without clothing. This is the antitheses of wearing your Sunday best, a doing away with the elaborate ritual attire often worn in other religions.

Many Wiccans—perhaps the majority—wear robes during ritual. Some even enter the magic circle in street clothing. Others wear nothing.

Outsiders, on hearing of Wiccan ritual nudity, sneer and say, "See? They're naked during their rituals. That *proves* that they have orgies!"

This belief is the product of a prejudiced, unnatural state of mind. What could be more natural than the unclothed human body? As has been pointed out numerous times in the past, none of us are born wearing clothing.

Sociological studies of peoples around the world affirm that the use or non-use of clothing is a matter of local custom. What we (or any society) judge to be a decent coverage of the human body may be thought of as outrageously indecent in some other society.

The idea of practicing ritual nudity certainly isn't strictly Wiccan. AmerIndians, Polynesians, Amazonian Indians, Europeans, certain ethnic groups that settled in the United States, and many other peoples of various cultures have removed clothing for religious purposes. To this day in India, the *saddhus* are allowed to walk the streets naked as a symbol of their sanctity. It seems that our Western minds are quite closed when it comes to the sight of our own bodies.

Why is this? Pre-Christian cultures such as those of ancient Egypt, Greece, and Rome accepted social nudity. When Christianity came along, its early leaders equated nudity with earlier (Pagan) religions. Thus nudity—even while bathing—was firmly linked with the enemy of this religion and was roundly forbidden. At some times, even individuals in the privacy of their own homes weren't allowed to remove their clothing.

When social nudity disappeared as a common practice in the West, twisted ideas concerning it festered in the popular mind. Nudity is dirty, filthy. Nudity is evil. Nudity leads to sex. Sex is bad.

The false, unnatural belief that nudity is evil and inevitably leads to sex is the product of 1500 years of prudery, and it is fostered by a new religion determined to erase all traces of Paganism.

But any rational, well-adjusted person who has visited a nude beach, a clothing-optional resort or nudist camp realizes that nudity soon loses its novelty. When persons are naked for reasons other than sex, the arousal quotient of such a state quickly vanishes.

Some Wiccans claim that all their rituals in the past were conducted without clothing. This simply isn't true. Though there is much precedent for ritual nudity, most of Europe was far too cold for such practices.

Some Wiccans perform nude rituals because they see this as a natural state, the closest they can be to the Goddess and God. Others don't take off their clothing because they prefer not to. Far from ritual nudity being a requirement in Wicca, many Wiccans vehemently condemn the practice. When it is used, ritual nudity is engaged in for specific purposes, not for the titillation that rolls around in the minds of outsiders.

Wicca, as has been frequently mentioned, is a religion of individuals.

Now to the more explosive of these two issues—sex. Any mention of the word Witchcraft usually brings to mind orgies. Sex and Witchcraft, outsiders believe, are inextricably linked. As with many myths, this one simply isn't true.

A few—not many, but a few—Wiccan traditions do utilize sex for its mystical and magical properties and to alter consciousness.

But such rites—as rare as they are—are only performed in private between two consenting adults. Ritual sex is never engaged in before other Wiccans or anyone else. Coven orgies are nonexistent. Wicca is not a swing club; Sabbats and Esbats aren't excuses to have sex.

After all, most of us have enough excuses along these lines. Wiccans certainly don't need to hide behind their religion to make whoopee.

Those Wiccans (and they are in the minority, believe me!) that utilize sex have no apologies for doing so.

They see Wicca as a fertility religion, and so deem sex a natural component of its rituals. Centuries of Christian sexual repression, they say, is responsible for the public's horror of ritual sex, as well as of sex itself in any of its variant forms.

Our morals are thrust upon us by the society in which we live. Our society is dominated by the idea that sex should be engaged in only by married couples and solely for procreative purposes. Therefore, sex for any other reason is deemed sinful, even by married couples. In the public's mind, combining sex with religion is an abomination.

Wiccans could argue that it's really none of their business, but that wouldn't get anyone too far.

What most people don't understand is that there are sexual elements in every religion, even in Christianity. The Bible is filled with rapes and ritual intercourse. The very word "testament" derives from a practice that was quite common in Biblical times. When one man was swearing an oath to another he grasped his testicles. Most of the sexual aspects of Christianity have, of course, been covered up with confusing translations, or have been conveniently left out of the authorized versions of the Bible. But they are there.

So a few Wiccans may utilize sex as a joyous, energy-raising experience during ritual. But they do so only with their partner—generally within an established emotional relationship, such as that existing between husband and wife. Wicca is not a sex religion, and most Wiccans don't integrate sex into their rituals.

But what is sex really? Strip off those old bugaboos and prejudices and look at it: Sex is a union with self, with another individual, with the human race as a whole, and with the Deity or Deities that created us. One variety of sex is the first step toward the creation of human life. When viewed with an open mind, uncluttered by artificial morality, sexual rituals are indeed religious and sacred in the old pre-Christian sense of these words.

Wiccans don't believe that the pleasures and wonders of sex are unnatural or evil. They don't believe that the God and Goddess created sexuality as a test of the goodness of humans, and they truly can't conceive of such a thing. They see sex as a joyous part of life, and so some Wiccans celebrate this in ritual.

Wicca is a unique religion, one with great variety. The fact that sex (and ritual nudity) plays a role in *some* Wiccan covens and traditions doesn't mean that *all* Wiccans give it the same ritual importance.

Those that do see it as an act of love, power, and spirituality.

16

Dangers And Troubles

Every human being should have the right to practice any religion that he or she wishes. Though laws upholding freedom of religion have been enacted in many nations, many others continue to persecute those with certain religious beliefs. And indeed, legislation doesn't change popular opinion, as evidenced in the intervening years since the U.S. civil rights movement of the 1960s.

Religious persecution has been with us as long as there has been religion. Wars are still raging due to (at least in part) doctrinal differences. Many persons hide behind religion, using it as an excuse for greed, racism, sexism, bigotry, prejudice, and of course, murder. What should be a spiritually uplifting force has often been perverted and twisted to suit personal needs.

Religion is used as a weapon against other religions. This becomes clear as we view what has happened to Wicca in the last twenty years or so.

In Chapter One we looked at the reasons why many of the old Pagan traditions died out in Europe, as well as the uproar among orthodox religions when occultism experienced an upsurge of interest in the late 1960s. Even now, in the late 1980s, this controversy is still raging, often with increasingly violent effects.

As we've seen, Wiccans don't kill humans. They don't mutilate or kill animals. They don't sign pacts with Satan—in blood or in ink. They don't call up evil demons, and they're certainly not out to rule the world. All they desire is the freedom to practice their own religion.

In many cases, Wiccans are denied this simple, basic right. Stories originating from all parts of the country attest to the fact that when Wiccans are publicly known, they often suffer.

The reason for this, of course, is ignorance. The mass media delights in spreading misinformation concerning Wicca. Wiccans give interviews to the press and are symbolically burned at the stake for speaking of their religion. Articles about Wicca are rarely carried in the religious section of newspapers, and quotes from priests and ministers are often included in an attempt to malign the religion.

Would they end an article about an upcoming Jewish holiday with, say, a born-again Christian's diatribe against this religion?

Like many other Wiccans, I've been verbally assaulted while on television by snickering talk-show hosts and hostile audiences. We've suffered through hours of television specials portraying Wiccans as mentally deranged, twisted, Satanic murderers. One hour-long show aired recently on a major network attempted to link a positive Wiccan group with murder.

Despite the media's bigotry, certain Wiccan traditions have been recognized by the I.R.S. Department of Army Pamphlet No. 165-13, entitled "Religious Requirements and Practices of Certain Selected Groups—A Handbook for Chaplains" notifies Army personnel that Wiccans are as much entitled to religious rights as followers of any other religion. Many prisons also allow inmates to practice Wicca.

But such recognition is slow in coming. Though many televangelists have fallen from grace lately, those still in business often preach about the dangers of "Witches." A woman who had "infiltrated" a Wiccan coven appeared on such a show I watched a few years ago. She had attended rituals, read the books and periodicals, and had in every way been exposed to Wiccan philosophy and spirituality.

And yet she spent the entire show saying over and over again that Wiccans—she used that word—worship the Devil and are out to conquer the world.

Such blind faith, or conscious twisting of facts, has led to dangerous situations. A Wiccan coven in California decided to perform one of their rituals in a public park. This is a fairly common occurrence in urban areas. Well in advance of the ritual they had obtained the required meeting permit to avoid any unpleasant situations. The day arrived and the coven, wearing robes, set up their altar in full daylight and began their simple rite.

They cast a circle and invoked the Goddess and God. Halfway through the ritual, somebody saw them, sized up the situation from their point of view and called the police.

"Satanists!" the informer said in an agitated voice. "Human sacrifice. They're—they're killing babies in the park!"

Not long afterward several patrol cars pulled up, and law enforcement officers poured out. They rudely broke up the ritual and disturbed the tools on the altar while the astonished Wiccans helplessly looked on. Then the interrogations began. It could have been a scene out of the Middle Ages or the Renaissance, not California in the 1980s.

By the time the rightfully outraged Wiccans showed the officers their permit and convinced them that they were simply conducting a religious rite, and not a murder, the ritual area was a shambles. All thoughts of proceeding with the ritual, or even of beginning again, were quickly forgotten.

One person's willful, intentional lies had violently ended a Wiccan ritual. Because the call was anonymous, she or he was never charged with the crime of disturbing a religious ceremony.

Another variation on this theme occurred in the Midwest. A Wiccan group began hosting Esbats on their land in the countryside. Soon after news of their religious meetings spread, a staunch churchgoer decided that these persons were Satanists. People interviewed by local newspapers informed reporters that they were keeping their children inside on the nights of the Full Moon so that they wouldn't be killed by the Witches. Slanderous allegations spread through the rural community for several weeks, all directed against a nature-loving, life-affirming group that was legally recognized as a religious organization.

Such incidents are far from isolated. The persecution continues out of ignorance and deceit.

As we've seen, Wicca was once a secret religion. Its rituals were performed far from prying eyes, certainly not in public parks. Interested persons were sworn to secrecy, initiated, and trained.

Some of the reasons for this secrecy are clear, taking into account the above stories. Ignorant persons can wreak havoc for contemporary Wiccans. Four hundred years ago these groups would have been legally executed, an act that would have sent a warm glow of satisfaction through the populace. Even today, public disclosure of Wiccan membership can result in tragedy.

At least one Wiccan ended his life after his religion became publicly known through the actions of an unscrupulous outsider. This wasn't from shame but from the emotional, psychological, and financial persecution that resulted from this undesired and vicious revelation.

Being a Wiccan in this world isn't easy. Wiccans have been punched in the mouth and beaten on city streets for wearing pentagrams. They have been assaulted by rock-throwing "Christians."* Wiccans have been burned out of their homes. They've lost jobs, housing, husbands, and wives. Hate mail regularly arrives at their doors. Their children have been abducted by mates who misunderstood their religion.

Fundamentalist Christians picket outside Wiccan gatherings, and bomb threats are made. Occasionally Wiccans are even murdered for their religious

---

* I put quotes around this word because such persons certainly aren't following the teachings of Jesus.

beliefs. And over and over again they're accused of murder, Satan worship, cattle mutilation, child molestation, orgies, and even influencing the lyrics to rock and roll music.

Many outsiders say that Wiccan secrecy covers up what they're *really* doing. Again, old misconceptions die hard. In light of the real dangers awaiting publicly known Wiccans, there seems to be only one solution to the problem—education.

Tell the non-Wiccans what Wicca is about, many Wiccans are saying. Assure them that Wiccans are normal, everyday citizens who just happen to practice a different religion. Let them know the truth about Wicca.

Thus many Wiccans are emerging from the shadows. They write books about their religion, appear on television, and speak to the public about Wicca. Frankly, some of them enjoy the attention that is directed to them. After all, they're only human.

Many of them have been persecuted for their trouble. All have been rewarded by a slow but growing understanding of Wicca among the masses. Perhaps Wicca hasn't been accepted in the United States as a viable, alternative religion. Neither has Shintoism or Buddhism or many other ways unfamiliar to the West. But the groundwork has been laid, and is already providing positive results. The very fact that this book could be published and distributed is proof of that.

The Wiccans are speaking.

17

A Wiccan Ritual

Because rituals constitute the outward expression of religions, it might be illuminating to look at a basic Wiccan ritual. The following example is, once again, an excerpt from *Wicca: A Guide For The Solitary Practitioner.*

Wiccan rituals are varied. Particular Wiccan traditions have specific rituals that are often adhered to rigidly. Other nontraditional Wiccans may create new rituals for each occasion. And some groups (or individuals) perform spontaneous rites—chanting or moving or speaking as they feel compelled to do, using a few objects symbolic of the season.

Most Wiccan rituals follow the pattern outlined in the next few paragraphs. There are many variations; these are generalizations only.

Prior to the ritual, the celebrant may bathe to cleanse the physical body as well as the spiritual. The area to be used is often purified with incense, salt, or some other tool.

The ritual itself begins with the creation of sacred space—the magic circle. Next, the Goddess and God are invoked to witness the rites. *How* they're invoked is up to the group or individual involved. Most rely on words; others may chant, sing, make music, or dance. The form isn't important. What *is* important is that the invocations are successful in attuning the Wiccans with the Goddess and God.

Once they have been invoked, the actual workings begin. If the meeting is a Sabbat, a seasonal rite (such as the one below) is enacted. This may involve spoken passages, sacred plays, or dramatic demonstrations of the season's attributes.

If the ritual is an Esbat, an invocation is spoken, sung, or chanted to the Goddess in Her lunar aspect. A meditation may occur next, following by the magical workings. Scrying (the act of gazing into a crystal sphere, pool of water, candle flame) may follow. In a coven new initiates may be taught basic Wiccan techniques.

On Sabbats the seasonal rites precede the magic, if it is done at all. Afterward, some Wiccans practice various forms of divination. Samhain is one Sabbat at which this is traditional. Through divination, Wiccans seek glimpses of the coming winter months.

Following this is a simple ritual meal, sometimes known as Cakes and Wine or Cakes and Ale; in the below ritual it is termed The Simple Feast. The meal usually consists of wine, ale, or fruit juice, and crescent-shaped cakes. The cakes (actually cookies) are more commonly found at Esbats. Bread may also be substituted.

Far from mocking the Christian communion, Wiccans are following the forms of ancient Middle Eastern and Greek rituals in which such meals—including the crescent cakes—were enjoyed. The ritual meal also echoes the wild feasts once held during agricultural rituals in rural Europe two or three hundred years ago.

It is widely known that Christianity borrowed ritual practices of earlier traditions when it was being organized. Ask any theologian about the veracity of this statement.

After the meal the magic sphere is "broken" or "opened." This is the ceremonial dispersing of the power that created it. When a coven gathers for a Sabbat, a feast often occurs after the ritual.

Here, then, is the Standing Stones Tradition's Mabon Sabbat ritual. It is celebrated on the Autumn Equinox, the exact date of which varies from around the 19th to the 23rd of September each year. It is symbolic of the second harvest, when winter is settling in, and the fertility of the Earth diminishes with each sunset. The God, echoing the waning of the growing season, prepares for death.

Here is the ritual in full, with comments in parentheses where necessary:

Mabon

Decorate the altar with acorns, oak sprigs, pine and cypress cones, ears of corn, wheat stalks, and other fruits and nuts. Also place there a small rustic basket filled with dried leaves of various colors and kinds. (These are representations of the season, as well as manifestations of the bounty which the Goddess and the God have produced.)

Arrange the altar, light the candles and censer, and cast the Circle of Stones (Chapter Twelve).

The Blessing Chant:

> *May the powers of The One*
> *The source of all creation;*
> *all-pervasive, omnipotent, eternal;*
> *may the Goddess,*
> *the Lady of the Moon*
> *and the God,*
> *Horned Hunter of the Sun;*
> *may the powers of the Spirits of the Stones,*
> *rulers of the elemental realms;*
> *may the powers of the stars above and the*
> *Earth below,*
> *bless this place, and this time, and I who am*
> *with you.*

(The "One" mentioned in the first line is the ultimate source of energy out of which the Goddess and God were created. It is the power of the universe, the life-force, the Cosmic Matrix. This chant, [which isn't really chanted], is usually said while standing before the altar.)

Invoke the Goddess and God:

> ### *Invocation To The Goddess:*
>
> *Crescent One of the starry skies,*
> *Flowered One of the fertile plain,*
> *Flowing One of the ocean's sighs,*
> *Blessed One of the gentle rain;*
> ***Hear** my chant 'midst the standing stones,*

Open me to Your mystic light;
Waken me to Your silver tones;
Be with me in my sacred rite!

Invocation To The God:

Ancient God of the forest deeps,
Master of beast and Sun;
Here where the world is hushed and sleeps
Now that the day is done.
I call You in the ancient way
Here in my circle round,
Asking that You will hear me pray
And send Your Sun-force down.

(These are two suggested invocations. Many others can be used, or can be composed on the spot.)

Stand before the altar, holding aloft the basket of leaves, and slowly scatter them so that they cascade to the ground within the circle. Say words such as these:

Leaves fall,
the days grow cold.
The Goddess pulls Her mantle of Earth
around Her
as you, O Great Sun God, sail toward the
West
to the lands of eternal enchantment,
wrapped in the coolness of night.
Fruits ripen,
seeds drop,
the hours of the day and night are balanced.
Chill winds blow in from the North wailing
laments.

> In this seeming extinction of nature's power,
>   O Blessed Goddess,
> I know that life continues.
> For spring is impossible without the second
>   harvest,
> as surely as life is impossible without death.
> Blessings upon You, O Fallen God,
>   as you journey into
> the lands of winter and into the Goddess'
>   loving arms.

(West is symbolically seen here as the direction of death. This is because the Sun and Moon both "die" there each day.)

Place the basket down and say:

> O Gracious Goddess of all fertility,
> I have sown and reaped the fruits of my actions,
> good and bane.
> Grant me the courage to plant seeds of joy
> and love in the coming year,
> banishing misery and hate.
> Teach me the secrets of wise existence upon
>   this planet,
> O luminous One of the night!

(A seasonal meditation usually follows here, during which the Wiccan contemplates the changing of the Earth, as well as the ways in which these changes are felt within her/himself. This may last for a minute or two, or for a longer period.)

Works of magic. (If any are necessary; but again, many Wiccans reserve the Sabbats for religious workings, and perform acts of magic during Esbats.)

The Simple Feast.

Between your hands, hold up a cup of wine or some other liquid to the sky and say:

> *Gracious Goddess of Abundance,*
> *Bless this wine and infuse it with Your love.*
> *In Your names, Mother Goddess and*
> *Father God,*
> *I bless this wine (or juice, etc.).*

Hold up a plate of crescent cakes (bread, biscuits) with both hands to the sky and say:

> *Powerful God of the Harvest,*
> *Bless these cakes and infuse them with Your love.*
> *In Your names, Mother Goddess and Father God,*
> *I bless these cakes (or this bread).*

The circle is released.

Mabon Lore

A traditional practice is to walk in wild places and forests, gathering seed pods and dried plants. Some of these can be used to decorate the home, others are saved for future herbal magic.

The foods of Mabon consist of the second harvest's gleanings, so grains, fruit, and vegetables predominate, especially corn. Corn bread is traditional fare, as are beans and baked squash.

This, then, has been an example of one type of Wiccan Sabbat ritual. Though it has been written for a solitary practitioner, two or more persons could easily enact it by dividing the parts. Group rituals don't differ much from this. In coven workings, four individuals may call the Spirits of the Stones (or Watchtowers) at the four quarters during the circle-casting. The basket of leaves could be handed around the coven so that each Wiccan scatters a few of them during the invocation. The crescent cakes may be blessed by a man, the wine by a woman.

Many of the books listed in the Bibliography contain Wiccan rites designed for group participation.

I think it's important to remember that such rituals represent only the outer form of Wicca. It is the processes at work within the Wiccan—the blossoming of the consciousness of the Goddess and God within, the attunement with the seasons, the flow of Earth energy through the body—that constitutes true Wicca.

Anyone could say these words and perform these actions and feel absolutely nothing. Just as in magic, it is the practitioner's intention which determines a religious ritual's effectiveness. If a person enacts this or any other Wiccan rite with the proper feeling, it can, and will be, successful in creating a union between human, Earth, and the Goddess and God.

I can't see how anything in the above ritual would threaten anyone else. I can't understand how Wicca could be construed as a threat to anyone or any organization. In its essence, Wicca is one with all other religions.

§

PART III

A SUMMARY

§

18

Consciousness Rises

A few years ago a man wrote a book about runes. His publisher ingeniously packaged the short book with a set of small ceramic squares etched with runes. The item, introduced just before Christmas as a gift set, sold beyond anyone's wildest dreams.

Shirley MacLaine, a famous actress, singer, and dancer, wrote the latest installment of her multivolume autobiography and introduced much of the United States to the doctrine of reincarnation. A later book—as well as a television miniseries based on it—brought the concept of channelling to millions of people.

Morning talk shows, newspapers, and *Time* magazine discussed the energies lying within crystals. Stockbrokers and lawyers revealed that they kept large quartz crystals in their offices.

People around the world recently gathered at "power spots" and "vortexes" to experience the "Harmonic Convergence," and the press covered it extensively with their ubiquitous sarcasm and humor.

Just a few days ago, as I write this, a book was published that revealed that Nancy Reagan consults an astrologer. From 1981-1988 she ran the White House and President Reagan's appointments by the stars.

Everywhere around us, people are opening their minds. Long-forgotten practices are being dusted off and examined for possible contemporary uses. Persons are investigating the powers of the mind, of the Earth, of stones and herbs. Many are looking at past lives, searching for clues to unlock the mysteries of our existence.

Consciousness is indeed arising. Orthodox religions—those that teach that the world is evil and illusory, that human beings have no power, or hope of achieving anything beyond peace within their Deity—are losing ground. Hundreds of thousands are expanding their lives and their world-views.

What has been termed the New Age has arrived. In some ways it's a high-tech echo of the occult renaissance that occurred from 1966 to 1974 in the United States and Great Britain. Powerful marketing campaigns are bringing age-old tools such as tarot decks, rune-stones, and crystals to millions of new and interested customers.

Many tools and processes have been embraced by the New Age—channelling, crystals, rebirthing, herbs, pyramid power, past-life regression, meditation, neuro-linguistic programming, yoga, and a host of others. Some of these are spiritual, some are psychological and others are magical in nature. But try to call a New Age person a Witch, or even a magician, and you're likely to be ridiculed and decried as a close-minded person.

However, traces of folk magic are alive in the New Age. Crystal workers, who usually engage in healing practices, are using age-old forms of folk magic. Persons who burn incense or otherwise utilize herbs are also following ancient rites. Pyramid power uses artificially constructed devices to concentrate the energy of the Earth. Though persons who work with these tools may not call themselves magicians, they are.

Recently, a woman came up to me after I'd taught a class in crystal magic. Smiling, she explained to me that she'd been using stones for healing others for several years. "I always wondered what magic was all about. Now I realize I've been practicing it all along," she said.

Magic wasn't what she'd expected. She didn't know that it was the process of moving natural energies to manifest needed goals. Not everyone involved in the New Age performs such acts, but many of them do.

Wiccans and folk magicians aren't necessarily partakers of New Age consciousness. They existed long before the media buildup occurred, and will be around after the excitement and megadollars have gone. To some outsiders though, they're all one and the same—enemies of "true" religion.

Magicians and Wiccans are drawn to "Old Age" tools and rituals. They don't necessarily channel entities. To many of them, the New Age is a watered-down version of ancient magical and spiritual processes which use the mechanized tools of the computer age. Many particularly decry the rising prices of such things as stones and herbs, as interest in them increases.

Despite this, it's certain that all this excitement has nudged many materialists into expanding their intellectual and spiritual horizons. New Age ideas have opened new avenues to vistas filled with wonders and occult ("hidden") knowledge, and have turned people's eyes away from their LCD watches and compact disc players to the mysteries of life and the Earth. In this sense, the New Age has certainly had a profound impact on contemporary American society.

Though some persons let go of their earlier prejudices and take up the practice of folk magic or Wicca, many of them still cling to quasi-Christian symbolism. They may attend "Christian" Spiritualist churches, or meditate upon the image of Jesus as a crystal while using its magic. The word "God" (capital G, with its unexpressed concept of male divinity) is frequently used in New Age books. Stores catering to this movement often fail to stock magical texts.

This is fine and understandable. Those from traditional religious backgrounds often find it hard to let go of Christian symbolism, even when they've found the more conventional forms of it less than satisfying. By holding on to religious motifs while performing New Age practices, they're creating new forms of religious magic.

Wiccans and folk magicians welcome the renewed interest in spirituality and magic in whatever forms it manifests. They also hope that with the spread of New Age consciousness, more people will come to understand, or at least tolerate, alternate religious and spiritual systems.

But Wiccans are not out to convert others. They agree that persons should find peace within their own religions. Those who can't move on to other traditions, seeking the correct combination of elements that allows them to feel that they consist of more than bones and flesh and a mind.

For some, this search leads to the simple splendor of folk magic. For others, to the religion of Wicca.

In what kind of world will the heirs of the New Age live? What will folk magicians and Wiccans find in the coming years, in the new century ahead?

Hopefully, they'll exist in a spiritually integrated society which provides for practitioners of all religious and magical paths; a world in which no one religion seeks to dominate and destroy all others in a vain attempt to prove its superiority.

True, we're human, with all the faults that this suggests. But perhaps at some time in the near future, we'll begin to realize that the forms of religious and spiritual practices are unimportant so long as they facilitate relationships between human beings and the Divine.

Perhaps the current wave will awaken the majority of persons to the spiritual reality of the physical world. Perhaps it will enhance the desire to preserve our planet by halting mindless, blind development and the misuse of life-threatening technology such as nuclear power.

If the New Age achieves nothing else, it will have done its work.

19

Toward The Light

This book's stated purpose is to explode the myths and superstitions regarding Wicca and magic, as well as to show just what Witchcraft is. It's not a religious tract intended to convert readers—it simply speaks the truth about folk magic and the Wiccan religion, with the hoped-for goal of spreading tolerance.

Though Wicca doesn't proselytize, and folk magicians don't look for new practitioners of the magical arts, many persons seek further information on these topics. Hence, I've included some guidelines in this chapter.

If, after reading this book, you wish to learn more about Wicca and magic, the best way to start is by reading. Read every book you can find on these subjects—both the good works and the bad. Read with a critical eye, evaluating each author individually. Be especially careful when reading books containing numerous Biblical quotations. These are certainly

written by nonpractitioners, and are filled with countless inaccuracies and downright lies.

Wicca

Remember that few Wiccans agree with one another
regarding ritual practices. The same is true of Wiccan
authors. Few Wiccan traditions are in complete agree-
ment with the methods of others. Because authors
write what they know best, each book may seem to
represent "true" Wicca, even though the authors' descriptions of the religion are totally different. Though
they're all members of the same religion, they are still
individuals. Wicca is a personal religion.

However, to be sure that the "Witchcraft" about
which you're reading is real, keep in mind the information contained within this book. If an author writes
of Satan worship, human sacrifices, forced initiations,
orgies, meals of human infants and other unpleasant
things, he or she is not a Wiccan, and the book is the
product of a twisted mind. Think of such books as
works of fiction or propaganda, because that's exactly
what they are.

You may decide that you wish to learn more. If so,
try to find a Wiccan in your area. Few Wiccans publicly
advertise or reveal their addresses, so it can be difficult to meet one. If you're serious about practicing
Wicca, seek out every lead you can find.

Write to authors of Wiccan books. Though you
may not get a reply, information can occasionally be
passed on that may help you. It's certainly worth the
time and effort.

Be careful. If you do contact someone through
rather strange means and are told that you will soon

become a true Satanist, that you have to renounce your former religion, and that you have to pay for initiation or take drugs to participate in ceremonies, then you're not in contact with a Wiccan coven or practitioner. Keep on looking.

If you meet a Wiccan individual or coven that practices ritual nudity or teaches sex magic, and this bothers you, simply reject them and look for another. The same is true if you feel a severe personality clash with any of the Wiccans you meet. Chances are they won't accept you anyway, for covens are small and good relationships between all members are essential to effective workings.

If you fail in your attempts to meet Wiccans, you may wish to begin practicing the religion alone. Check the Bibliography for books which contain whole or partial rituals, and put together some simple rites. Work at gathering together the tools. Mark the Sabbats and Esbats on your calendar, and start observing them as best you can.

Folk Magic

Most books on this subject—except for historical surveys—contain fairly accurate information. But even here strange rituals often appear. Many modern folk-magic books contain spells designed to manipulate others, or even to kill enemies. Such books are written to appeal to the lowest, basest desires in readers. The driving motivation for doing this is money. The authors who write such dangerous words often haven't had much experience, if at all, in magic.

So even if an author tells you, step-by-step, how to control another person, with no warnings of the consequences, keep in mind the basic magical doctrine of "harm none." You might reread Chapter Four of this book if you feel tempted to perform one of these acts.

If you wish to practice folk magic, that's easy enough. Read some of the books mentioned in the Bibliography and simply start doing so! You need no initiations to begin experiencing the powers of nature and the energy contained within your own body.

In Summary

Witches, people will tell you, are ugly old women who've sold their souls to the Devil, who work to destroy Christianity, who kill their babies and eat lizards for lunch. Additionally, it's believed that Witches belong to an organized, Satan-worshipping church.

Many individuals still believe that such bizarre persons actually did, and still do, exist. Five hundred years ago there may have been a few women who fit this image—crazed individuals who, with nothing else to strike out at, turned against conventional religion and their own families. Through a mixture of fantasy and psychosis, they became the characters that Christianity had invented. But as we've seen, they weren't Witches.

To sum up: Witchcraft today is folk magic—a gentle, ancient, constructive use of little-understood forces to effect positive change. This term also includes Wicca, a modern religion rooted in reverence of the Goddess and God, with a deep respect for nature. Magic and reincarnation are accepted parts of this religion, which has various traditions.

Folk magic isn't cursing, hexing, blasting, or any other negative magic. It isn't performed with powers derived from the Devil or from Satan.

Wicca isn't a parody, reversal, or perversion of Christianity. It isn't an evangelical, controlling, or proselytizing religion or cult. Wicca isn't out to rule the world, to convert your children, to take your money, or to force you to believe as its followers do. Wicca isn't anti-Christian; it's simply non-Christian.

Orgies and murders aren't a part of Witchcraft practices. These ideas are spread by persons who simply don't know the facts, or who choose to ignore the truth for their own ends. Wiccans and folk magicians don't wish to be feared or converted; they just want to be left alone.

It's time for us to throw off our prejudices and look at the ends of Witchcraft: spiritual attainment and a healthy, happy, financially secure life. Where's the horror in this? Where are the terrors that have fueled a thousand-thousand sermons, and that even today, contribute to religious murders?

The horror exists only in the minds of those who don't know the truth, and this lack of knowledge creates fear. Such fear is fueled by representatives of other religions, who use it to boost their memberships.

Folk magic and Wicca are gentle, loving ways of life practiced by hundreds of thousands of people. This *is* the truth about Witchcraft today.

Glossary

Italicized terms within the body of each discussion refer to other related entries in the glossary.

Akasha: The fifth element—the omnipresent spiritual power that permeates the universe. It is the energy out of which the *Elements* formed.

Athame: A Wiccan ritual knife. It usually has a double-edged blade and a black handle. The athame is used to direct *Personal Power* during *Ritual* workings. It is seldom (if ever) used for actual physical cutting. The term, of obscure origin, has many variant spellings among Wiccans and an even greater variety of pronunciations. American East Coast Wiccans may pronounce it as "ah-THAM-ee" (to rhyme with "whammy"); I was first taught to say "AHTH-ah-may," and later "ah-THAW-may."

Beltane: A Wiccan Sabbat celebrated on April 30th or May 1st (traditions vary). Beltane is also known as May Eve, Roodmas, Walpurgis Night, Cethsamhain. Beltane celebrates the symbolic union, or "marriage," of the Goddess and God, and links in with the approaching summer months.

Book of Shadows: A Wiccan book of rituals, spells, and magical lore. Once hand-copied upon *Initiation*, the B.O.S. is now photocopied or typed in some *Covens*. No one true Book of Shadows exists; all are relevant to their respective users.

Censer: A heat-proof container in which incense is smoldered. An incense burner. It symbolizes the *Element* of Air.

Charge, To: To infuse an object with *Personal Power*. An act of *Magic*.

Circle, Magic: *See Magic Circle.*

Circle of Stones: *See Magic Circle.*

Conscious Mind: That part of our minds which is at work while we balance our checkbooks, theorize, communicate, and perform other acts related to the physical world. Compare with *Psychic Mind*.

Coven: A group of Wiccans, usually initiatory and centering around one or two leaders, that gathers for religious and magical workings.

Craft, The: *Wicca. Witchcraft. Folk Magic.*

Days of Power, The: *See Sabbat.*

Deosil: Clockwise, or the direction in which the shadow on a sundial moves as the Sun "moves" across the sky. In northern hemisphere magic, deosil movement is symbolic of life, positive energies, good. It is much used in spells and rituals: i.e., "walk deosil around the Circle of Stones." Some Wiccan groups below the equator, notably in Australia, have switched from deosil to *Widdershins* motions in their rituals. *See also Widdershins.*

Divination: The magical art of discovering the unknown by interpreting random patterns or symbols. Tools such as clouds, tarot cards, flames, or smoke are used. Divination contacts the *Psychic Mind* by tricking or drowsing the *Conscious Mind* through *Ritual*, and by observing or manipulating tools. Divination isn't necessary for those who can easily attain communication with the psychic mind, although they may practice it.

Elements, The: Earth, Air, Fire, Water. These four essences are the building blocks of the universe. Everything that exists (or that has potential to exist) contains one or more of these energies. The elements hum within ourselves and are also "at large" in the world. They can be utilized to cause change through *Magic*. The four elements formed from the primal essence or power—*Akasha*.

Esbat: A Wiccan ritual usually occurring on the Full Moon and dedicated to the Goddess in Her lunar aspect.

Evocation: Calling up spirits or other nonphysical entities to either visible appearance or invisible attendance. This isn't a Wiccan practice. Compare with *Invocation*.

Folk Magic: The practice of projecting *Personal Power*, as well as the energies within natural objects such as herbs and crystals, to bring about needed change.

Imbolc: A Wiccan Sabbat celebrated on February 2nd, also known as Candlemas, Lupercalia, Feast of Pan, Feast of Torches, Feast of the Waxing Light, Oimelc, Brigit's Day and many other names. Imbolc celebrates the first stirrings of spring and the recovery of the Goddess from giving birth to the Sun (the God) at *Yule*.

Initiation: A process whereby an individual is introduced or admitted into a group, interest, skill, or religion. It is often undergone by a candidate of Wicca. Initiations may be ritual occasions but can also occur spontaneously.

Invocation: An appeal or petition to a higher power (or powers), such as the Goddess and God. A prayer. Invocation is actually a method of establishing conscious ties with those aspects of the Goddess and God that dwell within us. In essence, then, we seemingly cause them to appear, or make themselves known, by becoming aware of them.

Labrys: A double-headed axe which symbolized the Goddess in ancient Crete, and still used by some Wiccans for this same purpose. The two axe-heads represent the Goddess in Her Lunar aspect.

Lughnasadh: A Wiccan Sabbat celebrated on August 1st, also known as August Eve, Lammas, Feast of Bread. Lughnasadh marks the first harvest, when the fruits of the Earth are cut and stored for the dark winter months, and the God mysteriously weakens as the days grow shorter.

Mabon: A Wiccan Sabbat occurring on or around September 21st, the Autumnal Equinox, Mabon is a celebration of the second harvest, when nature prepares for winter. Mabon is a vestige of ancient harvest festivals which, in some form or another, were once nearly universal among peoples of the Earth, and still exists in the United States under the guise of the Thanksgiving holiday.

Magic: The projection of natural energies (such as *Personal Power*) to create needed change. Energy exists within all things: ourselves, plants, stones, colors, sounds, movements. Magic is the process of rousing this energy, giving it purpose, and releasing it. Magic is a natural, not supernatural, practice, but is little understood.

Magic Circle, The: A sphere constructed of *Personal Power* in which Wiccan rituals are usually enacted. The term refers to the circle that marks the sphere's penetration of the ground, for the sphere extends both above and below the surface of the ground. It is created through *Visualization* and *Magic*.

Meditation: Reflection, contemplation—turning inward toward the self, or outward toward Deity or nature. A quiet time in which the practitioner may either dwell upon particular thoughts or symbols or allow them to come unbidden.

Midsummer: The Summer Solstice, usually occurring on or near June 21st. One of the Wiccan festivals, and an excellent night for *Magic*. Midsummer marks the time of the year when the Sun (the God) is symbolically at the height of its powers. The longest day of the year.

Old Ones, The: A Wiccan term sometimes used to encompass all aspects of the Goddess and God.

Ostara: Occurs around March 21st, at the Spring Equinox. Ostara marks the beginning of true, astronomical spring, when snow and ice make way for green. As such, Ostara is a Fire and fertility Sabbat, celebrating the return of the Sun, the God, and the fertility of the Earth (the Goddess).

Pagan: From the Latin *paganus*, meaning country dweller. Today it is used as a general term for followers of Wicca and other magical and polytheistic religions. It is also used to refer to pre-Christian religious and magical systems. Naturally, Christians have their own negative definition of this word.

Pentacle: A ritual object (usually a circular piece of wood, metal, clay, etc.) upon which a five-pointed star (*Pentagram*) is inscribed, painted, or engraved. It represents the *Element* of Earth. The words "pentagram" and "pentacle" are not interchangeable, though they may understandably cause confusion.

Pentagram: The basic interlaced five-pointed star, visualized with one point upward. The pentagram represents the five senses, the *Elements* (Earth, Air, Fire, Water, and *Akasha*), the hand, and the human body. It is a protective symbol known to have been in use since the days of old Babylon. Today it is frequently associated with *Wicca*. A symbol of power.

Personal Power: That energy which sustains our bodies. It originates within the Goddess and God. We first absorb it from our biological mother within the womb, and later from food, water, the Moon and Sun, and other natural objects. We release it during movement, exercise, sex, conception, and childbirth. *Magic* is a movement of personal power for a specific goal.

Psychic Mind: The subconscious, or unconscious mind, in which we receive psychic impressions. The psychic mind is at work when we sleep, dream, and meditate. It is our direct link with the Divine, and with the larger, nonphysical world around us. Other related terms: *Divination* is a ritual process which utilizes the *Conscious Mind* to contact the psychic mind. Intuition is a term used to describe psychic information that unexpectedly reaches the conscious mind.

Psychism: The act of being consciously psychic, in which the *Psychic Mind* and *Conscious Mind* are linked and working in harmony. Also known as psychic awareness. *Ritual Consciousness* is a form of psychism.

Reincarnation: The doctrine of rebirth. The process of repeated incarnations in human form to allow evolution of the sexless, ageless soul. One of the tenets of *Wicca*.

Ritual: Ceremony. A specific form of movement, a manipulation of objects or inner processes designed to produce desired effects. In religion ritual is geared toward union with the Divine. In *Magic* it produces a specific state of consciousness that allows the magician to move energy toward needed goals. A *Spell* is a magical ritual.

Ritual Consciousness: A specific, alternate state of awareness necessary to the successful practice of magic. The magician achieves this consciousness through the use of *Visualization* and *Ritual*. It is an attunement of the *Conscious Mind* with the *Psy-*

chic Mind, a state in which the magician senses energies, gives them purpose and releases them toward the magical goal. It is a heightening of the senses, an expanded awareness of the nonphysical world, a linking with nature and with the forces behind all conceptions of Deity.

Runes: Stick-like figures, some of which are remnants of old Teutonic alphabets. Others are pictographs. These symbols are once again widely being used in *Magic* and *Divination*.

Sabbat: A *Wiccan* festival. See *Beltane, Imbolc, Lughnasadh, Mabon, Midsummer, Ostara, Samhain* and *Yule* for descriptions.

Samhain: A Wiccan Sabbat celebrated on October 31st, also known as November Eve, Hallowmass, Halloween, Feast of Souls, Feast of the Dead, Feast of Apples. Samhain marks the symbolic death of the Sun God and His passing into the "land of the young," where He awaits rebirth of the Mother Goddess at Yule. This Celtic word is pronounced by Wiccans as "SOW-wen" (the "sow" sounds like the first three letters in sour); "SEW-wen"; "SAHM-hain"; "SAHM-ain"; "SAV-een" and other ways. The first pronunciation seems to be the one preferred by most Wiccans.

Scry, To: To gaze at or into an object (a quartz crystal sphere, pool of water, reflections, a candle flame) to still the *Conscious Mind* in order to contact the *Psychic Mind*. This practice allows the scryer to become aware of events prior to their actual occurrence, as well as to perceive past or present events through other than the five senses. A form of *Divination*.

Simple Feast, The: A *Ritual* meal shared with the Goddess and God.

Spell: A magical *Ritual*, usually nonreligious in nature and often accompanied by spoken words.

Spirits Of The Stones, The: The elemental energies naturally inherent within the four directions of the Earth. They are personified within the *Standing Stones Tradition* as the "Spirits of the Stones," and in other Wiccan traditions as the "Lords of the Watchtowers." They are linked with the *Elements*.

Talisman: An object charged with *Personal Power* to attract a specific force or energy to its bearer.

Tradition, Wiccan: An organized, structured, specific Wiccan subgroup, which is usually initiatory, often with unique ritual practices. Many traditions have their own *Books of Shadows*, and usually recognize members of other traditions as Wiccan. Most traditions are composed of a number of *Covens* as well as solitary practitioners.

Visualization: The process of forming mental images. Magical visualization consists of forming images of needed goals during *Ritual*. Visualization is also used to direct *Personal Power* and natural energies for various purposes during *Magic*, including *Charging* and forming the *Magic Circle*. It is a function of the *Conscious Mind*.

White-Handled Knife: A normal cutting knife with a sharp blade and white handle. It is used within Wicca to cut herbs and fruits, to slice bread during *The Simple Feast*, and for other functions—but never for sacrifice. Sometimes called the bolline. Compare with *Athame*.

Wicca: A contemporary *Pagan* religion with spiritual roots in the earliest expressions of reverence of nature. Some of its major identifying motifs are: reverence for the Goddess and the God; acceptance of reincarnation and magic; ritual observance of astronomical and agricultural phenomena; and the creation and use of spheroid temples for ritual purposes.

Widdershins: Anti-clockwise motion, usually used in the Northern Hemisphere for negative magical purposes, or for dispersing negative energies or conditions such as disease. Southern Hemisphere Wiccans may use widdershins motions for exactly the opposite purposes; namely, for positive ends. In either case, widdershins and deosil motions are *symbolic*; only strict, close-minded traditionalists believe that accidentally walking around the altar backwards, for instance, will raise negativity. Their use in Wicca stems from ancient European rituals practiced by peoples who watched and reverenced the Sun and Moon in their daily revolutions. Widdershins motions, within ritual contexts, are still shunned by the majority of Wiccans, though some use it while, for instance, dispersing the *Magic Circle* at the end of a rite.

Witch: In ancient times, a practitioner of the remnants of pre-Christian folk magic, particularly that kind relating to herbs, stones, wells, rivers, and stones. One who practiced *Witchcraft*. Later, this term's meaning was deliberately altered to denote a

demented, dangerous, supernatural being who practiced destructive magic—a threat to Christianity.
This change in meaning was a political, monetary,
and sexist move on the part of organized religion—
not a change in the practices of Witches. This later,
erroneous meaning is still accepted by many non-
Witches. It is also used by some members of *Wicca*
to describe themselves.

Witchcraft: The *craft* of the *Witch*—*Magic*, especially
magic utilizing *Personal Power* in conjunction with
the energies within stones, herbs, colors, and other
natural objects. (*See Folk Magic.*) By just using this
definition, Witchcraft isn't a religion. However, some
followers of *Wicca* use this word to denote their
religion. Yes, it is a bit confusing.

Yule: A *Wiccan* Sabbat celebrated on or about December 21st, marking the rebirth of the God from
the Goddess. A time of joy and celebration during
the miseries of winter. Yule occurs at the Winter
Solstice.

Annotated Bibliography

Many books on Wicca and folk magic have been written. Many of them are good, but the vast majority are poor. I've grouped recommended books into sections according to their main points of interest, and have added short notes describing the book's contents.

Be aware that just because a book is included here doesn't mean that I, Wiccans, or folk magicians agree with everything said within it. Remember—read discriminatingly.

Though many of these books are out of print, they can still be found in used bookstores and libraries, and some are being reprinted.

Folk Magic

Bowman, Catherine. *Crystal Awareness*. St. Paul: Llewellyn Publications, 1987.
A New Age handbook of crystal magic.

Buckland, Raymond. *Practical Color Magick*. St. Paul: Llewellyn Publications, 1983.
Folk magic and color.

Buckland, Raymond. *Practical Candle Burning*. St. Paul: Llewellyn Publications, 1971.
A book of candle magic that has become one of the standard guides.

Burland, C. A. *The Magical Arts: A Short History*. New York: Horizon Press, 1966.
A history of British and European folk and ceremonial magic. Complete with photographs.

Chappel, Helen. *The Waxing Moon: A Gentle Guide To Magic*. New York: Links, 1974.
A delightful look at herbs, stones, and other tools of folk magic. One chapter describes Wicca. Ignore the Satanic references.

Devine, M. V. *Brujeria: A Study Of Mexican-American Folk Magic*. St. Paul: Llewellyn Publications, 1982.
Contemporary Mexican-American folk and religious magic. This book describes an eclectic form of Wicca, well-mixed with Catholicism and ancient Mexican magic.

Gonzalez-Wippler, Migene. *The Complete Book of Spells, Ceremonies And Magic*. New York: Crown, 1977. Reprint. St. Paul: Llewellyn Publications, 1988.
Truly an overview of the magical arts, this book contains a wealth of traditional folk spells, as well as a look at the ceremonies and techniques of ceremonial magic. A source book for all forms of magic. Many photographs and illustrations.

Malbrough, Ray T. *Charms, Spells And Formulas For The Making And Use Of Gris-Gris, Herb Candles, Doll Magick, Incenses, Oils And Powders*. St. Paul: Llewellyn Publications, 1986.
Cajun folk magic. The title says it all.

Mickaharic, Draja. *Spiritual Cleansing: A Handbook Of Psychic Protection*. York Beach, Maine: Weiser, 1982.

Folk magic techniques for purification and protection garnered from around the world.

Valiente, Doreen. *Natural Magic*. New York: St. Martin's Press, 1975.
The magic of herbs, stones, and other interesting information. This book has recently been reprinted.

Weinstein, Marion. *Positive Magic: Occult Self-Help*. New York: Pocket Books, 1978.
A classic, thoughtful, enlightened guide to folk magic. Contains an insightful chapter on Wicca. An enlarged version has been published.

Worth, Valerie. *The Crone's Book Of Words*. St. Paul: Llewellyn Publications, 1971, 1986.
A charming collection of unusual and original folk magic spell-poems.

Ceremonial Magic

Agrippa, Henry Cornelius. *The Philosophy Of Natural Magic*. Antwerp, 1531. Reprint. Chicago: de Laurence, 1919. Reprint. Secaucus: 1974.
This work contains the first volume of Agrippa's Three Books of Occult Philosophy. Later additions, which are rather quaint, are also included.

Agrippa, Henry Cornelius. *Three Books Of Occult Philosophy*. 1533. First English translation published London, 1651. Reprint. London: Chthonios Books, 1986.
This book is the first publication of Agrippa's complete magical work in over 300 years. It contains much of the magical lore of his time—particularly that concerning plants, animals, stones, the planets

and elements. I've included it in this section because it contains much ceremonial magic as well as folk magic.

Barrat, Francis. *The Magus: A Complete System Of Occult Philosophy.* 1801. New Hyde Park: 1967.
This book culls much of the magical material that had been published in one form or another up until 1800.

Junius, Manfred M. *Practical Handbook Of Plant Alchemy.* New York: Inner Traditions International, 1985.
A look at the "lesser work" of laboratory alchemy, a magical art.

Kraig, Donald. *Modern Magick.* St. Paul: Llewellyn Publications, 1988.
A how-to course for the student who wishes to learn the practice of ceremonial magic.

Mathers, S. L. MacGregor, ed. and trans. *The Key Of Solomon The King.* New York: Weiser, 1972.
One editor's version of a classic magical text, pieced together from various manuscript copies.

Regardie, Israel. *The Golden Dawn.* St. Paul: Llewellyn Publications, 1971.
A classic manual detailing group magical workings.

Shah, Sayed Idries. *The Secret Lore Of Magic.* New York: Citadel, 1970.
Extracts from various magical texts.

Shah, Sirdal Ikbal Ali. *Occultism: Its Theory And Practice.* New York: Castle Books, n.d.
More selections from old magical texts.

Thompson, C. J. S. *The Mysteries And Secrets Of*

Magic. New York: The Olympia Press, 1972.
This fascinating work contains extracts of rare, un-
published magical texts.

Mythology, Folklore And The Goddess

Bord, Janet and Colin. *Earth Rites: Fertility Practices In
Pre-Industrial England.* Salem Acad., 1983.
Survival of Pagan customs in the post-Christian era.
A fascinating glimpse into the past.

Cirlot, J. E. *A Dictionary Of Symbols.* New York: Philo-
sophical Library, 1962.
Ancient religious and magical symbolism.

Dexter, T. F. G. *Fire Worship In Britain.* New York:
Macmillan, 1931.
Pagan customs surrounding the solstices, equinoxes,
and other feast days in pre-WWII Britain are explored in this charming booklet.

Downing, Christine. *The Goddess: Mythological Images
Of The Feminine.* New York: Crossroad, 1984.
One of the first of the wave of new books con-
cerning the Goddess.

Frazer, Sir James. *The Golden Bough.* New York: Macmillan, 1956 (one-volume abridged edition).
A classic study of rites and religions from around
the world. The information is sound; some of Sir
Frazer's conclusions are not.

Graves, Robert. *The White Goddess.* New York: Farrar,
Straus and Giroux, 1973.
A poetic look at the Goddess. Considered a classic
by many modern Wiccans, it has had a great in-

fluence.

Harding, Esther. *Women's Mysteries: Ancient And Modern.* New York: Pantheon, 1955.
Women and spirituality.

Harley, Timothy. *Moon Lore.* Tokyo: Charles E. Tuttle Co., 1970.
Mythology and legend surrounding the Moon.

Leach, Maria, and Jerome Fried, eds. *Funk And Wagnalls Standard Dictionary Of Folklore, Mythology And Legend.* New York: Funk and Wagnalls, 1972.
A monumental collection of mythic and ritual information. Thousands of articles on subjects such as plants, crystals, goddesses and gods.

Newmann, Erich. *The Great Mother: An Analysis Of The Archetype.* Princeton: Princeton University Press, 1974.
A scholarly survey of various aspects of the Goddess by a Jungian.

Stone, Merlin. *When God Was A Woman.* New York: Dial Press, 1976.
A feminist (woman-centered) look at spirituality in past times.

Walker, Barbara. *The Women's Encyclopedia Of Myths And Mysteries.* San Francisco: Harper & Row, 1983.
An encyclopedia of ancient religion and Goddess worship.

Contemporary Wicca

Adler, Margot. *Drawing Down The Moon: Witches, Druids, Goddess-Worshippers And Other Pagans In America Today.* New York: Viking, 1979.
   An inside, informed look at Wicca and Paganism. An updated version has recently been published. Photographs.

Buckland, Raymond. *Witchcraft From The Inside.* St. Paul: Llewellyn Publications, 1971.
   One of the earliest American books on Wicca, this is an explication of so-called "Gardnerian" Wicca. Photographs.

Buckland, Raymond. *Witchcraft . . . The Religion.* Bay Shore, New York: The Buckland Museum of Witchcraft and Magick, 1966.
   An early pamphlet describing Gardnerian Wicca.

Deutch, Richard. *The Ecstatic Mother: Portrait Of Maxine Sanders—Witch Queen.* London: Bachman & Turner, 1977.
   A written portrait of Maxine Sanders (see Sanders, Maxine below) by a Wiccan author. Photographs.

Gardner, Gerald. *The Meaning Of Witchcraft.* London: Aquarian Press, 1959, 1971.
   Gerald Gardner's look at the origins of Wicca. Photographs.

Gardner, Gerald. *Witchcraft Today.* London: Rider, 1954. New York: Citadel, 1955.
   This book was the first to be written by a Witch (read: Wiccan). It is therefore of great importance. The author describes various aspects of Gardnerian Wicca—as much as he dared at the time—including

the tools, ritual nudity, magic, the magic circle, and many other topics. Complete with photographs. Remember, this book describes Wicca solely from Gardner's point of view.

Glass, Justine. *Witchcraft: The Sixth Sense And Us*. North Hollywood: Wilshire, 1965.
An early look at the symbolism and lore of various traditions of British Wicca (most notably The Regency). It also explores psychic phenomena. Photographs.

Johns, June. *King Of The Witches: The World Of Alex Sanders*. New York: Coward McCann, 1969.
A mythological biography of the founder of Alexandrian Wicca, once one of the most prevalent traditions of Wicca. Photographs.

Leek, Sybil. *The Complete Art Of Witchcraft*. New York: World Publishing, 1971.
This book, by one of the most famous Witches of the past decade, describes a nontraditional, eclectic Wiccan system. Photographs.

Leek, Sybil. *Diary Of A Witch*. New York: Prentice-Hall, 1968.
The book that introduced Witches and Wicca to much of the United States when it became a best seller in the late 1960s. An autobiography of a British Wiccan.

Martello, Leo L. *Witchcraft: The Old Religion*. Secaucus: University Books, 1973.
An offbeat look at Wicca, with particular emphasis on Italian Witch-lore.

Roberts, Susan. *Witches USA*. New York: Dell, 1971.

Reprint. Hollywood: Phoenix House, 1974.
This book, one of the first surveys of the Wiccan
scene in the early 1970s, caused quite a stir among
Wiccans when it was republished. However, it stands
as a delightful (though somewhat dated) look at
Wicca, and contains no more inaccuracies than any
other book of its type.

Sanders, Maxine. *Maxine The Witch Queen*. London:
Star Books, 1976.
Yet another Wiccan autobiography—this one by
the woman who, with her then-husband Alex Sanders, began the Alexandrian Wiccan movement. Includes many interesting behind-the-scenes stories
of her activities with Alex. Photographs.

Valiente, Doreen. *An ABC Of Witchcraft Past And Present*. New York: St. Martin's Press, 1973.
An encyclopedia of Gardnerian Wiccan lore and
mostly British folklore. Quite useful and fun to
read.

Valiente, Doreen. *Where Witchcraft Lives*. London:
Aquarian Press, 1962.
This book, written by the author before she had
publicly acknowledged herself as a Witch, is filled
with Sussex folklore as well as stories of Wiccan
rituals and bits of folk magic.

Practical Wiccan Books
And Ritual Manuals

Buckland, Raymond. *The Tree: The Complete Book Of
Saxon Witchcraft*. New York: Weiser, 1974.
The first modern Wiccan tradition to have been

written specifically for publication in its entirety. Useful to those studying the religion. It was written after Buckland broke from the Gardnerian tradition.

Buckland, Raymond. *Buckland's Complete Book of Witchcraft.* St. Paul: Llewellyn Publications, 1986.
A unique workbook containing fifteen "lessons," constituting a study-course in Wicca. Though drawn from various traditions, it relies mainly on the Seax (Saxon) Wicca tradition published in the above entry. Along the way Buckland also covers such topics as meditation, rites of passage, divination, herbalism, runes, and healing. Lesson Fifteen is devoted to the solitary practitioner.

Budapest, Z. *The Feminist Book Of Light And Shadows.* Venice, California: Luna Publications, 1976.
A feminist ritual book which has been quite influential and has started numerous new traditions. A revised version of this book, as well as a second volume, have also been published under the names *The Holy Book Of Women's Mysteries.* Vols. 1 & 2.

Crowther, Patricia. *Lid Off The Cauldron: A Handbook For Witches.* London: Frederick Mueller, 1981.
This book, by one of Gerald Gardner's initiates, contains detailed instructions on the magic circle, Sabbat rituals, symbolism, tools and "calls" (or sonics), and a chapter on Gerald Brosseau Gardner.

Farrar, Janet and Stewart. *Eight Sabbats For Witches.* London: Robert Hale, 1981.
These onetime Alexandrian Wiccans provide their own Gardnerian-based Sabbat rituals, along with a circle-casting, and birth, marriage and death rituals.

Heavily Irish-based. Includes inside information from Doreen Valiente concerning the sources of Gerald Gardner's ritual system. Photographs.

Farrar, Janet and Stewart. *The Witches' Way*. London: Robert Hale, 1985.
Further revelations, courtesy of Doreen Valiente, concerning the composition of the Gardnerian Wiccan rituals. Includes many extracts of once secret rituals, as well as many of the authors' own rites. Photographs.

Farrar, Stewart. *What Witches Do*. New York: Coward, McCann and Geoghegan, 1971.
The first book to reveal Wiccan rituals, it outlines much of the philosophy and practices of Alexandrian Wicca. This system is based on Gardnerian practices. Photographs.

Fitch, Ed. *Magical Rites From The Crystal Well*. St. Paul: Llewellyn Publications, 1984.
A compilation of Pagan rituals written by Mr. Fitch for a now defunct magazine that had great impact on Wiccans a decade ago.

K., Amber. *How To Organize A Coven Or Magical Study Group*. Madison, Wisconsin: Circle Publications, 1983.
An intelligent guide to doing just that.

Lady Sheba. *The Book Of Shadows*. St. Paul: Llewellyn Publications, 1971.
This much-contested book is one (not "the") ritual book. Again, based on the Gardnerian tradition.

Lady Sheba. *The Grimoire Of Lady Sheba*. St. Paul:

Llewellyn Publications, 1974.
Spells, herbal recipes, and more revelations of traditional Gardnerian Wicca scattered here and there.

Slater, Herman, ed. *A Book Of Pagan Rituals.* New York: Samuel Weiser, 1978.
Rituals of The Pagan Way, an early Pagan (almost Wiccan) organization. Rites for the Sabbats, magical information and so on.

Starhawk. *The Spiral Dance: A Rebirth Of The Ancient Religion Of The Great Goddess.* San Francisco: Harper & Row, 1979. One of the most influential books ever published on Wicca. This nontraditional, feminist book contains numerous rituals and fine exercises designed to strengthen magical abilities, as well as to fine-tune spiritual awareness.

Stein, Diane. *The Women's Spirituality Book.* St. Paul: Llewellyn Publications, 1987.
A source book of women's spirituality, including philosophy, Goddess traditions, and Sabbat rituals. Various aspects of folk magic such as healing and crystals are also included.

Valiente, Doreen. *Witchcraft For Tomorrow.* London: Robert Hale, 1978.
Another book by Doreen Valiente, this one was written to allow non-initiates to practice Wicca. In the first eleven chapters she covers everything from ancient British mythology to sex magic. Part two contains a Wiccan ritual system that was written specifically for this book. It lacks only Sabbat rituals. Photographs.

Weinstein, Marion. *Earth Magic: A Dianic Book Of Shad-*

ows. New York: Earth Magic Productions, 1980.
A unique, intriguing guide to practicing Wicca. An
expanded version has also been published.

STAY IN TOUCH

On the following pages you will find listed, with their current prices, some of the books now available on related subjects. Your book dealer stocks most of these, and will stock new titles in the Llewellyn series as they become available. We urge your patronage.

To obtain a FREE COPY of our latest full CATALOG of New Age books, tapes, videos, products and services, just write to the address below. In each 80-page catalog sent out bimonthly, you will find articles, reviews, the latest information on New Age topics, a listing of news and events, and much more. It is an exciting and informative way to stay in touch with the New Age and the world. The first copy will be sent free of charge and you will continue receiving copies as long as you are an active customer. You may also subscribe to *The Llewellyn New Times* by sending a $5.00 donation ($20.00 for overseas). Order your copy of *The Llewellyn New Times* today!

The Llewellyn New Times
P.O. Box 64383-Dept. 127, St. Paul, MN 55164

TO ORDER BOOKS AND PRODUCTS ON THE FOLLOWING PAGES:

If your book dealer does not carry the titles listed on the following pages, you may order them directly from Llewellyn. Please send full price in U.S. funds, plus $1.50 for postage and handling for orders *under* $10.00; $3.00 for orders *over* $10.00. There are no postage and handling charges for orders over $50. UPS Delivery: We ship UPS whenever possible. Delivery guaranteed. Provide your street address as UPS does not deliver to P.O. Boxes; UPS to Canada requires a $50 minimum order. Allow 4-6 weeks for delivery. Orders outside the USA and Canada: Airmail—add retail price of book; add $5 for each non-book item (tapes, etc.); add $1 per item for surface mail. You may use your major credit card to order these titles by calling 1-800-THE-MOON, M-F, 8:00-5:00, Central Time. Send orders to:

LLEWELLYN PUBLICATIONS
P.O. BOX 64383-127
St. Paul, MN 55164-0383, U.S.A.

Prices subject to change without notice.

EARTH POWER
by Scott Cunningham

Magick is the art of working with the forces of Nature to bring about necessary, and desired, changes. The forces of Nature—expressed through Earth, Air, Fire and Water—are our "spiritual ancestors" who paved the way for our emergence from the prehistoric seas of creation. Attuning to, and working with these energies in magick not only lends you the power to effect changes in your life, it also allows you to sense your own place in the larger scheme of Nature. Using the "Old Ways" enables you to live a better life, and to deepen your understanding of the world about you. The tools and powers of magick are around you, waiting to be grasped and utilized. This book gives you the means to put Magick into your life, shows you how to make and use the tools, and gives you spells for every purpose.

0–87542–121–0, 176 pgs., 5-1/4 x 8, illus., softcover $8.95

MAGICAL HERBALISM: The Secret Craft of the Wise
by Scott Cunningham

In *Magical Herbalism*, certain plants are prized for the special range of energies—the vibrations, or powers—they possess. *Magical Herbalism* unites the powers of plants and man to produce, and direct, change in accord with human will and desire.

This is the Magic of amulets and charms, sachets and herbal pillows, incenses and scented oils, simples and infusions and anointments. It's Magic as old as our knowledge of plants, an art that anyone can learn and practice, and once again enjoy as we look to the Earth to rediscover our roots and make inner connections with the world of Nature.

This is the Magic of Enchantment . . . of word and gesture to shape the images of mind and channel the energies of the herbs. It is a Magic for everyone—for the herbs are easily and readily obtained, the tools are familiar or easily made, and the technology that of home and garden. This book includes step-by-step guidance to the preparation of herbs and to their compounding in incense and oils, sachets and amulets, simples and infusions, with simple rituals and spells for every purpose.

0–87542–120–2, 256 pgs., 5-1/4 x 8, illus., softcover $7.95

Prices subject to change without notice.

HERB MAGIC VIDEO
by and featuring Scott Cunningham

Herb Magic, written by and featuring Scott Cunningham, gives the clearest view ever of how to do magic with herbs!

- Watch Scott prepare magical oils, sachets, incenses, and more.
- Visit a large, working herb farm.
- Learn to identify common herbs.
- Discover and use the power of herb magic and spells.
- Learn to make flower and herb essences, oils, and tinctures, bath oils or perfumes.

In this hour-long video, Scott presents many recipes and spells which use herbs. He gives specific, in-depth instructions on harvesting and preparing herbs for magical purposes. It is often easier to learn something by having it demonstrated to you. With this videotape Cunningham gives you a personal lesson in herb magic!

0-87542-117-2, VHS, 60 min. $29.95

CUNNINGHAM'S ENCYCLOPEDIA
OF MAGICAL HERBS
by Scott Cunningham

This is not just another herbal for medicinal uses of herbs—this is the most comprehensive source of herbal data for magical uses ever printed! Almost every one of the over 400 herbs are illustrated, making this a great source for herb identification. For each herb you will also find: magical properties, planetary rulerships, genders, associated deities, folk and Latin names and much more. To make this book even easier to use you will also find a folk name cross reference, and all of the herbs are fully indexed. There is also a large annotated bibliography, and a list of mail order suppliers so you can find the books and herbs you need.

Like all of Scott's books, this one does not require you to use complicated rituals or expensive magical paraphernalia. You will be able to discover which herbs, by their very nature, can be used for luck, love, success, money, divination, astral projection, safety, psychic self-defense and much more.

0-87542-122-9, 352 pgs., 6 x 9, illus., softcover $12.95

Prices subject to change without notice.

BUCKLAND'S COMPLETE BOOK OF WITCHCRAFT
by Raymond Buckland, Ph.D.

Here is the most complete resource to the study and practice of modern, non-denominational Wicca. This is a lavishly illustrated, self-study course for the solitary or group. Included are rituals, exercises for developing psychic talents, and information on all major "sects" of the Craft, sections on tools, beliefs, dreams, meditations, divination, herbal lore, healing, ritual clothing and much, much more. This book unites theory and practice into a comprehensive course designed to help you develop into a practicing Witch, one of the "Wise Ones." It is written by Dr. Ray Buckland, a very famous and respected authority on witchcraft who first came public with "the Old Religion" in the United States. Large format with workbook-type exercises, profusely illustrated and full of music and chants.

0–87542–050–8, 272 pgs., 8-1/2 x 11, illus., softcover $14.95

PRACTICAL CANDLEBURNING RITUALS
by Raymond Buckland, Ph.D.

Another book in Llewellyn's Practical Magick series. Magick is a way in which to apply the full range of your hidden psychic powers to the problems we all face in daily life. We know that normally we use only 5 per cent of our total powers—Magick taps powers from deep inside our psyche where we are in contact with the Universe's limitless resources. Magick need not be complex—it can be as simple as using a few candles to focus your mind, a simple ritual to give direction to your desire, a few words to give expression to your wish.

This book shows you how easy it can be. Here is Magick for fun, Magick as a Craft, Magick for Success. Love, Luck, Money, Marriage, Healing; Magick to stop slander, to learn truth, to heal an unhappy marriage, to overcome a bad habit, to break up a love affair, etc.

Magick—with nothing fancier than ordinary candles, and the 28 rituals in this book (given in both Christian and Old Religion versions)—can transform your life.

0–87542–048–6, 189 pgs., 5-1/4 x 8, illus., softcover $6.95

CUNNINGHAM'S ENCYCLOPEDIA OF
CRYSTAL, GEM & METAL MAGIC
by Scott Cunningham

Here you will find the most complete information anywhere on the magical qualities of over 75 crystals and gemstones as well as several metals. The information includes:

The Energy of Each Gem, Crystal or Metal, The Planet(s) Which Rule(s) the Crystal, Gem or Metal, The Magical Element (Air, Earth, Fire, Water) Associated with the Gem, Crystal or Metal , The Deities Associated with Each, The Tarot Card Associated with Each, The Magical Powers each Crystal, Metal and Stone are believed to Possess.

Also included is a complete description of how to use each gemstone, crystal and metal for magical purposes.

This is the book everyone will want to have! This is the book everyone will be quoting. This will be the classic on the subject.

0-87542-126-1, 6 x 9, 27 color plates, softcover.   **$12.95**

CHARMS, SPELLS AND FORMULAS
by Ray Malbrough

Hoodoo magick is a blend of European techniques and the magic brought to the New World by slaves from Africa. Hoodoo is a *folk magic* that can be learned and easily mastered by anyone.

By using the simple materials available in Nature, you can bring about the necessary changes to greatly benefit your life and that of your friends. You are given detailed instructions for making and using the *gris-gris* (charm) bags only casually or mysteriously mentioned by other writers. Malbrough not only shows how to make gris-gris bags for health, money, luck, love and protection from evil and harm, etc., but he also explains how these charms work. He also takes you into the world of *doll magick;* using dolls in rituals to gain love, success, or prosperity. Complete instructions are given for making the dolls and setting up the ritual.

0-87542-501-1, 192 pages, 5¼ x 8, illus., softcover   **$6.95**

WICCA: A GUIDE FOR THE SOLITARY PRACTITIONER
by Scott Cunningham

Wicca is a book of life, and how to live magically, spiritually, and wholly attuned with Nature. It is a book of sense and common sense, not only about Magick, but about religion and one of the most critical issues of today: how to achieve the much needed and wholesome relationship with out Earth. Cunningham presents Wicca as it is today—a gentle, Earth-oriented religion dedicated to the Goddess and God. This book fulfills a need for a practical guide to solitary Wicca—a need which no previous book has fulfilled.

Here is a positive, practical introduction to the religion of Wicca, designed so that any interested person can learn to practice the religion alone, anywhere in the world.

This book presents the theory and practice of Wicca from an individual's perspective. The section on the Standing Stones Book of Shadows contains solitary rituals for the Esbats and Sabbats. Exercises designed to develop magical proficiency, a self-dedication ritual, herb, crystal and rune magic, recipes for Sabbat feasts, are included in this excellent book.

0–87542–118–0, 240 pgs., 6 x 9, illus., softcover   **$9.95**

PRACTICAL COLOR MAGICK
by Raymond Buckland

Raymond Buckland has produced a fascinating and useful book which shows you how to reintroduce color into your life to benefit your physical, mental and spiritual well-being! Learn the secret meanings of color. Use color to change the energy centers of your body. Heal yourself and others through light radiation. Discover the hidden aspects of your personality through color.

This book will teach all the powers of light and more. You'll learn new forms of expression of your innermost self, new ways of relating to others with the secret languages of light and color. Put true color back into your life with the rich spectrum of ideas and practical magical formulas from *Practical Color Magick!*

0–87542–047–6, 136 pgs., 5-1/4 x 8, illus., softcover   **$6.95**

Prices subject to change without notice.

THE LLEWELLYN ANNUALS
Llewellyn's MOON SIGN BOOK: Approximately 400 pages of valuable information on gardening, fishing, weather, stock market forecasts, personal horoscopes, good planting dates, and general instructions for finding the best date to do just about anything! Articles by prominent forecasters and writers in the fields of gardening, astrology, politics, economics and cycles. This special almanac, different from any other, has been published annually since 1906. It's fun, informative and has been a great help to millions in their daily planning. **State year $4.95**

Llewellyn's SUN SIGN BOOK: Your personal horoscope for the entire year! All 12 signs are included in one handy book. Also included are forecasts, special feature articles, and an action guide for each sign. Monthly horoscopes are written by Gloria Star, author of Optimum Child , for your personal Sun Sign and there are articles on a variety of subjects written by well-known astrologers from around the country. Much more than just a horoscope guide! Entertaining and fun the year around. **State year $4.95**

Llewellyn's DAILY PLANETARY GUIDE and ASTROLOGER'S DATEBOOK: Includes all of the major daily aspects plus their exact times in Eastern and Pacific time zones, lunar phases, signs and voids plus their times, planetary motion, a monthly ephemeris, sunrise and sunset tables, special articles on the planets, signs, aspects, a business guide, planetary hours, rulerships, and much more. Large 5-1/4 x 8 format for more writing space, spiral bound to lay flat, address and phone listings, time zone conversion chart and blank horoscope chart. **State year $6.95**

Llewellyn's ASTROLOGICAL CALENDAR: Large wall calendar of 48 pages. Beautiful full-color cover and full-color inside. Includes special feature articles by famous astrologers, and complete introductory information on astrology. It also contains a Lunar Gardening Guide, celestial phenomena, a blank horoscope chart, and monthly date pages which include aspects, Moon phases, signs and voids, planetary motion, an ephemeris, personal forecasts, lucky dates, planting and fishing dates, and more. 10 x 13 size. Set in Central time, with fold-down conversion table for other time zones worldwide. **State year $9.95**

Prices subject to change without notice.

THE MAGIC IN FOOD
Legends, Lore & Spellwork
by Scott Cunningham

Foods are storehouses of natural energies. Choosing specific foods, properly preparing them, eating with a magical goal in mind: these are the secrets of *The Magic of Food*, an age-old method of taking control of your life through your diet.

Though such exotic dishes as bird's-nest soup and saffron bread are included in this book, you'll find many old friends: peanut butter and jelly sandwiches . . . scrambled eggs . . . tofu . . . beer. We've consumed them for years, but until we're aware of the energies contained within them, foods offer little more than nourishment and pleasure.

In *The Magic of Food* you'll learn the mystic qualities of everyday dishes, their preparation (if any) and the simple method of calling upon their powers. The author has included numerous magical diets, each designed to create a specific change within its user: increased health and happiness, deeper spirituality, enhanced sexual relations, protection, psychic awareness, success, love, prosperity . . . all through the hidden powers of food.

Filled with obscure recipes, fascinating lore and practical spells that you can do in the privacy of your own home, *The Magic in Food* is a book like no other!

0–87542–130–X, 384 pgs., 6 x 9, illus., color plates   **$14.95**

THE MAGICAL HOUSEHOLD
by Scott Cunningham and David Harrington

Whether your home is a small apartment or a palatial mansion, you want it to be something special. Now it can be with *The Magical Household*. Learn how to make your home more than just a place to live. Turn it into a place of security, life, fun and magic. Here you will not find the complex magic of the ceremonial magician. Rather, you will learn simple, quick and effective magical spells that use nothing more than common items in your house: furniture, windows, doors, carpet, pets, etc. You will learn to take advantage of the intrinsic power and energy that is already in your home, waiting to be tapped. You will learn to make magic a part of your life. The result is a home that is safeguarded from harm and a place which will bring you happiness, health and more.

0–87542–124–5, 208 pgs., 5-1/4 x 8, illus., softcover   **$8.95**

Prices subject to change without notice.

LLEWELLYN ORDER FORM
LLEWELLYN PUBLICATIONS
P.O. Box 64383-127, St. Paul, MN 55164-0383

You may use this form to order and of the Llewellyn books or products listed in this publication.

Give Title, Author, Order Number and Price.

_____

_____

_____

_____

_____

Be sure to add $1.50 for postage and handling ($3.00 for orders over $10.00). Minnesota residents add 6.5% sales tax. Outside USA add retail price of book for air mail; add $5 for non-book items. Add $1 per item for surface mail. You may charge on your ☐ VISA, ☐ MasterCard, or ☐ American Express.

Account No. _____

Exp. Date _____ Phone _____

Signature _____

Name _____

Address _____

City, State, Zip _____

_____

CHARGE CARD ORDERS (minimum $15.00) may call 1-800-THE-MOON during regular business hours, Monday-Friday, 8:00 am-4:30 pm CST. Other questions please call 612-291-1970.

☐ Please send me your FREE CATALOG!

Prices subject to change without notice.